HANNIBAL

MAKERS OF HISTORY SERIES

THE MAKERS OF HISTORY SERIES *includes:*

Nero
Alexander the Great
Hannibal
Julius Caesar

More titles forthcoming!

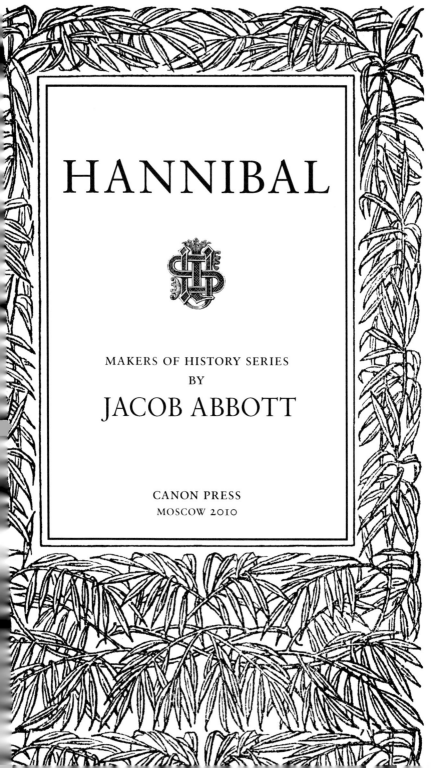

HANNIBAL

MAKERS OF HISTORY SERIES

BY

JACOB ABBOTT

CANON PRESS

MOSCOW 2010

Published in the year 2010 by
CANON PRESS
P.O. Box 8729, Moscow, ID 83843
800.488.2034 | www.canonpress.com

Hannibal by JACOB ABBOTT.
First printed in 1849.
Cover design by RACHEL HOFFMANN.
Cover photoshoppery by DAVID DALBEY.
Interior design by LAURA STORM.
Updated for the present day reader by
LUCY ZOE JONES.
Copyright © 2010 by CANON PRESS.

The "IHS" Christogram on the title page is an ancient
symbol used in the early Western church and is derived from the first
three letters of Jesus' name in the Greek alphabet. The first use of "IHS"
in an English document was in 1377, in a printing of
the medieval classic, *Piers Plowman*.

Library of Congress Cataloging-in-Publication Data

Abbott, Jacob, 1803-1879.
  [History of Hannibal the Carthaginian]
  Hannibal / Jacob Abbott.
      p. cm. -- (Makers of history)
  ISBN-13: 978-1-59128-059-0 (pbk.)
  ISBN-10: 1-59128-059-1 (pbk.)
  1. Hannibal, 247-182 B.C.--Juvenile literature. 2. Punic War, 2nd,
218-201 B.C.--Juvenile literature. 3. Generals--Tunisia--Carthage
(Extinct city)--Biography--Juvenile literature. 4. Rome--History--
Republic, 265-30 B.C.--Juvenile literature. 5. Carthage (Extinct city)--
History--Juvenile literature. I. Title. II. Series.
  DG249.A13 2009
  937'.04092--dc20
  [B]
                                                    2008021964

        10 11 12 13 14 15 16   10 9 8 7 6 5 4 3 2 1

CONTENTS.

FOREWORD.

N the third century before the birth of Christ, Rome and Carthage clashed over control of the island of Sicily. This began a series of three wars between these two major powers that lasted from 264 B.C. to 146 B.C. These wars, known as the Punic Wars, were named after the Roman word for Phoenicians, since Carthage was originally established as a Phoenician colony. Although both powers were evenly matched in terms of strength, Rome won all three struggles.

As the saying goes, it is the winners who write the histories. So it was that Rome, in addition to her victories on the battlefields, won the right to write the defining accounts of those wars. The earliest sources for the life of Hannibal, the greatest Carthaginian general, are found in the histories of the Roman historian Livy and the pro-Roman Greek historian Polybius, both of whom celebrated Rome's victory over Carthage.

Even though the battlefield winners write and interpret the events, the losers often win the hearts of readers. What if, we wonder, King Harold I of England had defeated William of Normandy at the Battle of Hastings in 1066? Or what might have happened if General Robert E. Lee had won the battle of Gettysburg in July 1863? The noble warrior fighting for a lost cause—the underdog and risk taker—easily captures our imaginations. Such were men like King Harold, General Lee, and Hannibal Barca of Carthage.

The events of history are unchangeable. Past events are as solidly fixed as the laws of mathematics. Though our record of events might be flawed and interpretations might vary, historical facts cannot change. But from a human perspective, what happened is not what absolutely had to happen. History is filled with "might have beens." The smallest change of events could have changed everything else that followed. If Pharaoh's soldiers, rather than his daughter, had found the baby Moses, the outcome would have been drastically different. There is no end to thinking about alternative courses of history. Both professional historians and students enjoy thinking, "What if?"

From the Christian perspective, we know that things happen to fulfill God's purposes; therefore, Rome defeated Carthage because of God's plan. But if Carthage had won, then we would know that God had purposed that outcome as well. Our task as Christian students of history is to acknowledge both God's sovereign rule over history and the actions and choices made by people in history.

Hamilcar Barca, a general from the First Punic War (264 to 241 B.C.), commissioned his young son Hannibal Barca to wage undying enmity against Rome. Hannibal instigated the Second Punic War by attacking Roman allies in Spain. In this war he gained immortal fame and changed history, but he nearly succeeded in changing the course of history even more, for he nearly succeeded in defeating Rome. Whereas the First Punic War was caused by economic and territorial interests, the second war was driven by a desire for revenge. Hannibal proved to be a mighty instrument used to inflict that revenge.

After war broke out in Spain, Hannibal moved his army through what is now southern France and crossed over the Alps to invade Italy. His crossing of the Alps with an army of over 50,000 men (along with horses and elephants) is an epic and monumental story in itself. Yet the greater part of Hannibal's mission remained. For the next fifteen years, he and his troops roamed the Italian peninsula, defeating Roman armies, dividing Roman allies, and plundering Roman farms and cities.

Repeatedly, Hannibal went into battle outnumbered. His uncanny skills, use of cavalry attacks on the enemy's flanks, and sheer audacity won him battle after battle. Hannibal made wise use of the terrain and took advantage of the divided Roman command system. He put fear into the Roman people and dissension into the Roman government. The most fearful saying among the Romans was *Hannibal ad portas,* meaning "Hannibal is at the gates." By carefully choosing his battles and marshalling his forces, Hannibal managed to capture everything Roman except for the city of Rome itself. Yet all the time that Hannibal was winning battles, he was losing the war.

Hannibal could frighten or depress the Romans, but he could never suppress their will to survive. When horrendous reports of battlefield dead were announced in Rome, new recruits readily enlisted. When Hannibal's army was camped near Rome, the Romans defied him by auctioning off the land on which his army was camped. The land sold at a high price, which signified that the Romans believed the invaders were a temporary nuisance rather than a long-term threat.

This unveils what is surely the great lesson of the story of Hannibal and the Second Punic War. For fifteen years, Hannibal controlled portions of the Italian peninsula and threatened the whole Roman world. Had the Romans been subjected to depressing nightly news reports, opinion polls, and expert analyses, Rome's future would have looked doubtful. Hannibal's presence was a real threat for fifteen years, which might seem to be a lifetime to a teenager, but is but a moment in the lifespan of a nation. What matters in the long term is not the enemy at the gates or the grim statistics of battlefield casualties. What matters in the long term is the long term.

Hannibal's boldness wins our hearts. His tactics on the battlefield awe both the military expert and the young student of history. His willingness to risk his own life along with that of his army, like a gambler throwing his fortune on one turn of the wheel, shows Hannibal's confidence and competence as a general. Although he is consistently rated as one of the greatest military generals of history, in the end, Hannibal is one of history's losers.

The clever man does not rule history; nor does the passing fad, the momentary opinion, or the current trend determine the future. God rules past, present, and future. Through the centuries, the Christian Church witnessed persecutions, heresies, and setbacks that threatened to extinguish the light of truth. In the long term, the dangers subsided and the truth prevailed. Men like Augustine, Luther, Calvin, and Knox were men who labored for the long-term perspective.

In the long term, Rome triumphed over Carthage. In the end, Hannibal, long after the Third Punic War, ended his life by taking poison to evade capture by the Romans. Roman victory over Carthage paved the way for the future advent of a still greater kingdom, the Kingdom of God.

BEN HOUSE
Trinity Season 2009

CHAPTER I

THE FIRST PUNIC WAR.

ANNIBAL was a Carthaginian general. He acquired his great distinction as a warrior by his dangerous struggles with the Romans. Rome and Carthage grew up together on opposite sides of the Mediterranean Sea. For about one hundred years they waged against each other the most dreadful wars. There were three of these wars. Rome was successful in the end, and Carthage was entirely destroyed.

There was no real cause for any disagreement between these two nations. Their hostility to each other was mere rivalry and spontaneous hate. They spoke a different language; they had different origins; and they lived on opposite sides of the same sea. So they hated and devoured each other.

Those who have read the history of Alexander the Great, in this series, will remember the difficulty he experienced in besieging and subduing Tyre, a great maritime city situated about two miles from the shore on the eastern coast of the Mediterranean Sea. Carthage was originally founded by a colony from this city of Tyre, and it soon became a great commercial and maritime power like its mother. The Carthaginians built ships and explored all parts of the Mediterranean Sea. They visited all the nations along the coasts, purchased the commodities they had to sell, carried them to other nations, and sold them at great profit. They soon began to grow rich and powerful. They hired soldiers to fight their battles and began to take possession of the islands of the Mediterranean and, in some instances, of points on the mainland. For example, some of their ships travelling to Spain found that the natives had silver and gold, which they obtained from veins of ore near the surface of the ground. At first the Carthaginians obtained this gold and silver by selling commodities of various kinds to the natives, which they had procured in other countries; paying, of course, to the producers only a very small price compared with what they required the Spaniards to pay them. Finally, they took possession of that part of Spain where the mines were situated and worked the mines themselves. They dug deeper; they employed skillful engineers to make pumps to raise the water, which always accumulates in mines and prevents the mines from being worked to any great depth. They founded a city there, which they called New Carthage—*Nova Carthago*. They fortified the city with military posts and made it the center of their operations in Spain. This city is called Cartagena to this day.

Therefore, the Carthaginians did everything by the power of money. They extended their operations in every direction, each new extension bringing in new treasures and increasing their means of extending even more. They had, besides the merchant vessels which belonged to private individuals, great ships of war belonging to the state. These vessels were called galleys and were rowed by oarsmen, tier above tier, there being sometimes four and five banks of oars. They had armies too, drawn from different countries, in various troops, according to how the different nations excelled in the different methods of warfare. For instance, the Numidians, whose country extended in the neighborhood of Carthage, on the African coast, were famous for their horsemen. There were great plains in Numidia and good grazing, and it was, consequently, one of those countries in which horses and horsemen naturally thrive. On the other hand, the natives of the Balearic Isles, now called Majorca, Minorca, and Ibiza, were famous for their skill as slingers.

The tendency of the various nations to adopt and cultivate different methods of warfare was far greater in those ancient times than now. The Balearic Isles, in fact, received their name from the Greek word *ballein,* which means to throw with a sling. The youth there were trained to perfection in the use of this weapon from a very early age. It is said that mothers used to practice the plan of putting the bread for their boys' breakfast on the branches of trees, high above their heads, and not allow them to have their food to eat until they could bring it down with a stone thrown from a sling. So the Carthaginians, in making up their forces, would hire bodies of cavalry in Numidia and of slingers in the Balearic Isles; and for similar reasons, they got excellent infantry in Spain.

In this way the Carthaginian power became greatly extended. The whole government, however, was exercised by a small body of wealthy and aristocratic families at home. It was very similar to a government like that of Victorian England, only the aristocracy of England was based on ancient birth and landed property, whereas in Carthage it depended on commercial greatness, combined with hereditary family distinction. The aristocracy of Carthage controlled and governed everything. None but its own sons could obtain office or power. The great mass of inhabitants were kept in a state of servitude and subjection. The government of an oligarchy sometimes makes a very rich and powerful state, but a discontented and unhappy people. Such was the Carthaginian power at the time it commenced its dreadful conflicts with Rome.

Rome itself was very differently situated. It was built by some wanderers from Troy, and it grew, for a long time, silently and slowly, by a sort of internal principle of life and energy. One region after another of the Italian peninsula was merged in the Roman state. They formed a population which was stationary and agricultural. They tilled the fields; they hunted the wild beasts; they raised great flocks and herds. They seem to have been a race possessed of a very refined and superior organization, which, in its development, gave rise to a character of firmness, energy, and force, both of body and mind, which has justly gained the admiration of mankind. The Carthaginians had discernment—the Romans called it cunning—and activity, enterprise, and wealth. Their rivals, on the other hand, were characterized by genius, courage, and strength, giving rise to a certain calm and unconquerable resolution and energy, which has since, in every age, been strongly associated in the minds of men with the very word "Roman."

The progress of nations was much slower in ancient days than now, and these two rival empires continued their gradual growth and extension, each on its own side of the great sea which divided them, for five hundred years before they came into collision. At last, however, the collision came.

The island of Sicily is separated from the mainland by a narrow strait called the Strait of Messina. This strait derives its name from the town of Messina, which is situated on it, on the Sicilian side. Opposite Messina, on the Italian side, there was a town named Rhegium. Now it happened that both of these towns were taken over by lawless bodies of soldiers. The Romans came and delivered Rhegium and severely punished the soldiers who had seized it. The Sicilian authorities advanced to the deliverance of Messina. The troops there, finding themselves threatened, sent to the Romans requesting that they come and protect them, and offering in return to deliver Messina into their hands.

The question of what answer to give to the request was brought before the Roman senate, and caused them great confusion. It seemed inconsistent to take sides with the rebels of Messina, when they had punished so severely those of Rhegium. Still the Romans were becoming very jealous of the growth and extension of the Carthaginian power. Here was an opportunity to meet and resist it. The Sicilian authorities were calling for direct aid from Carthage to recover the city, and the situation would probably result in establishing a large body of Carthaginian troops within sight of the Italian shore, and at a point where it would be easy for them to make hostile incursions into the Roman territories. In a word, it was a case of political necessity; that is to say, a case in which the interests of one of the parties in a contest were so strong that all considerations of justice, consistency, and honor were sacrificed to promote them.

The contest for Messina was, after all, considered by the Romans merely as a pretext, or rather as an occasion, for starting the struggle which they had long desired. They displayed their characteristic energy and skill in the plan which they adopted at the outset. They knew that the power of Carthage rested mainly on her command of the seas and that they could not hope to successfully cope with her until they could meet and conquer her on her own territory. In the meantime, however, they had not a single ship and not a single sailor, while the Mediterranean was covered with Carthaginian ships and seamen. Not at all daunted by this extraordinary inequality, the Romans decided to begin at once the work of creating for themselves a naval power.

The preparations took quite some time; for the Romans not only had to build the ships, but they first had to learn *how* to build them. They took their first lesson from a Carthaginian galley which was cast away in a storm on the coast of Italy. They seized the galley, collected their carpenters to examine it, and set woodmen at work to cut trees and collect materials for imitating it. The carpenters studied their model very carefully, measured the dimensions of every part, and observed the manner in which the various parts were connected and secured together. The heavy shocks which vessels are exposed to from the waves make it necessary to secure great strength in the construction of them; and though the ships of the ancients were very small and imperfect, compared with the warships of the present day, it is still surprising that the Romans were able to succeed at all in such a hasty attempt at building them.

They did, however, succeed. While the ships were being built, officers appointed for the purpose were training men, on shore, in the art of rowing them. Benches, like the seats which the oarsman would occupy in the ships, were arranged on the ground, and the intended seamen were drilled every day in the movements and action of rowers. The result was that a few months after the building of the ships began, the Romans had a fleet of one hundred galleys of five banks of oars ready. They remained in harbor with them for some time, to give the oarsmen the opportunity to see whether they could row on the water as well as on the land, and then boldly put to sea to meet the Carthaginians.

One part of the arrangements made by the Romans in preparing their fleets was strikingly characteristic of the determined resolution which marked all their conduct. They constructed machines containing grappling irons, which they mounted on the prows of their vessels. The engines were designed so that the moment one of the ships that contained them should encounter a vessel of the enemy, the grappling irons would fall on the deck of the enemy ship and hold the two firmly together, so as to prevent the possibility of either escaping from the other. The idea that the Romans would have any wish to withdraw from the encounter seemed entirely out of the question. Their only fear was that the Carthaginian seamen would employ their superior skill and experience in naval maneuvers in making their escape. Mankind has always regarded the action of the Romans as one of the most striking examples of military courage and resolution which the history of war has ever recorded.

The result was as might have been expected. The Romans captured, sank, destroyed or chased away the Carthaginian fleet that came to oppose them. They took the prows of the ships which they captured, carried them to Rome, and built what is called a *rostral pillar* of them. A rostral pillar is a column decorated with prows, which were, in the Roman language, called *rostra*. This column was nearly destroyed by lightning about fifty years afterward, but it was repaired and rebuilt again. It stood for many centuries, a very striking and appropriate monument of this extraordinary naval victory. The Roman commander in this case was the consul Duilius, and the rostral column was erected in his honor.

The Romans now prepared to carry the war into Africa. Of course it was easy, after their victory over the Carthaginian fleet, to transport troops across the sea to the Carthaginian shore. The Roman commonwealth was governed at the time by a senate, who made the laws, and by two supreme executive officers called consuls. They thought it was safer to have two chief magistrates than one, as each of the two would naturally be a check or balance on the other. The result was, however, that mutual jealousy often involved them in disputes and quarrels. In modern times, it is thought that to have one chief magistrate in the state is best, and other methods are provided to put a check on any action he might take to abuse his powers.

The Roman consuls, in time of war, took command of the armies. The name of the consul on whom it fell to carry on the war with the Carthaginians, after this first great victory, was Regulus, and his name has been celebrated in every age on account of his extraordinary adventures in the military operations and his untimely fate. How far the story is strictly true it is now impossible to know, but the Roman historians relate the following story:

At the time when Regulus was elected consul he was a plain man, living simply on his farm, sustaining himself by his own work, and displaying no ambition or pride. His fellow citizens, however, observed those qualities of mind in him which they were accustomed to admire and made him consul. He left the city and took command of the army. He enlarged the fleet to more than three hundred vessels. He put one hundred and forty thousand men on board and sailed for Africa. One or two years were spent in making the preparations, during which time the Carthaginians had improved in building new ships; so that, when the Romans set sail and were moving along the coast of Sicily,

they soon came in sight of a larger Carthaginian fleet assembled to oppose them. Regulus advanced to the contest.
The Carthaginian fleet was beaten as before. The ships
which were not captured or destroyed made their escape
in all directions, and Regulus went on, without further opposition, and landed his forces on the Carthaginian shore.
He set up camp as soon as he landed and sent back word to
the Roman senate asking what was next to be done.

Now that the great difficulty and danger of driving
back the Carthaginian fleet was past, the senate ordered
Regulus to send home nearly all the ships and a large part
of the army and with the rest he was to continue his march
toward Carthage. Regulus obeyed: he sent back the troops
which had been ordered home and with the rest began to
advance on the city.

Just at that time, however, news came to him that the
farmer who was caring for his land at home had died, and
that his little farm, on which rested his sole reliance for the
support of his family, was going to ruin. Regulus sent word
to the senate, asking them to place someone else in command of the army and to allow him to resign his office that
he might go home and take care of his wife and children.
The senate sent back orders that he should go on with his
operation and promised to provide support for his family
and to see that someone was appointed to take care of his
land. This story is thought to illustrate the extreme sim-
plicity of all the habits of life among the Romans in those
days. It is, however, very extraordinary that a man who
was entrusted with the command of a fleet of a hundred
and thirty vessels and an army of a hundred and forty
thousand men, should have a family at home dependent for
subsistence on the hired cultivation of seven acres of land.
Still, such is the story.

Regulus advanced toward Carthage, conquering as he came. The Carthaginians were beaten in one field after another and were reduced to near ruin when an occurrence took place which changed the balance of power. This was the arrival of a large body of troops from Greece, with a Grecian general at their head. These were troops which the Carthaginians had hired to fight for them, as was the case with the rest of the army. But these were *Greeks,* and the Greeks possessed the same qualities as the Romans. The newly-arrived Grecian general quickly displayed such military superiority that the Carthaginians gave him the supreme command. He prepared the army for battle. He had one hundred elephants in the front division of the army. They were trained to rush forward and trample down the enemy. He had the Greek phalanx in the center, which was a close, compact body of many thousand troops, bristling with long, iron-pointed spears, with which the men pressed forward, bearing everything before them. Regulus was, in a word, ready to meet Carthaginians, but he was not prepared to encounter Greeks. His army was scattered and he was taken prisoner. Nothing could exceed the triumph in the city when they saw Regulus and five hundred other Roman soldiers brought in as captives. A few days before, they had been in terror at the imminent danger of his coming in as a ruthless and vindictive conqueror.

The Roman senate was not discouraged by this disaster. They fitted out new armies, and the war went on. Regulus was kept the whole time at Carthage as a prisoner. At last the Carthaginians authorized Regulus to go to Rome as a sort of commissioner, to propose to the Romans an exchange prisoners to make peace. They exacted from him a solemn promise that if he was unsuccessful he would return. The Romans had taken many of the Carthaginians as prisoners in their naval combats and held them captive at Rome. It is customary, in such cases, for the warring nations to make an exchange and restore the captives on both sides to their friends and home. It was such an exchange of prisoners as this which Regulus was to propose.

When Regulus reached Rome he refused to enter the city, but he appeared before the senate from outside the city walls, in a very humble garb and with the most subdued and unassuming demeanor. He was no longer, he said, a Roman officer, or even citizen, but a Carthaginian prisoner, and he disavowed all right to direct, or even to counsel, the Roman authorities in respect to the proper course to be pursued. Nevertheless, he offered his opinion and said that the Romans ought not to make peace or to exchange prisoners. He himself and the other Roman prisoners were old and infirm and not worth the exchange; moreover, they had no claim whatever on their country, as they could only have been made prisoners in consequence of want of courage or patriotism to die in their country's cause. He said that the Carthaginians were tired of the war and that their resources were exhausted. He suggested the Romans press forward in it with renewed vigor and leave himself and the other prisoners to their fate.

The senate very slowly and reluctantly decided to follow his advice. They all earnestly attempted to persuade Regulus that he was under no obligation to return to Carthage. His promise, they said, was extorted by the circumstances of the case and was not binding. Regulus, however, insisted on keeping his faith with his enemies. He sternly refused to see his family, and bidding the senate farewell, he returned to Carthage. The Carthaginians, exasperated that he intervened to prevent the success of their mission, tortured him for some time in the most cruel manner, and finally put him to death. One would think that he ought to have counseled peace and an exchange of prisoners, and not refused to see his unhappy wife and children; but it was certainly very noble of him to refuse to break his word.

The war continued for sometime longer, until finally, both nations became weary of the contest and made peace. The following is the treaty which was signed. It shows that the advantage, on the whole, in this first Punic war, was on the part of the Romans:

"There shall be peace between Rome and Carthage. The Carthaginians shall evacuate all of Sicily. They shall not make war upon any allies of the Romans. They shall restore to the Romans, without ransom, all the prisoners which they have taken from them and pay them within ten years three thousand two hundred talents of silver."

The war had continued twenty-four years.

CHAPTER II

HANNIBAL AT SAGUNTUM.

HE name of Hannibal's father was Hamilcar. He was one of the leading Carthaginian generals. He occupied a very prominent position because of his rank, wealth, and high family connections at Carthage, and also because of the great military strength which he displayed in the command of the armies abroad. He carried on the wars which the Carthaginians waged in Africa and in Spain after the conclusion of the war with the Romans, and he longed to commence hostilities with the Romans again.

At one time, when Hannibal was about nine years of age, Hamilcar was preparing to set off on an expedition into Spain, and as was usual in those days, he was celebrating the occasion with games and displays and various religious ceremonies. It has been the custom in all ages of the world, when nations go to war with each other, for each side to take measures to satisfy the wrath and win the favor of Heaven. Christian nations at the present day do it by prayers offered for the success of their troops. Heathen nations do it by sacrifices and offerings. Hamilcar made arrangements for such sacrifices, and the priests were offering them in the presence of the whole assembled army.

Young Hannibal was present. He was a boy of great spirit and energy, and he entered into the scene with much enthusiasm. He wanted to go to Spain with the army, and he went to his father and began to make his request. His father would not consent to it. He was too young to endure the lack of basic necessities and fatigues of such an adventure. However, his father brought him to one of the altars, in the presence of the other officers of the army, and made him lay his hand on the consecrated victim and swear that, as soon as he was old enough and had it in his power, he would make war on the Romans. This was done, no doubt, in part to amuse young Hannibal's mind and to relieve his disappointment in not being able to go to war at that time, by promising him a great and mighty enemy to fight at some future day. Yet Hannibal remembered it and longed for the time to come when he could go to war against the Romans.

Hamilcar bid his son farewell and departed for Spain. He extended his conquests there in all directions west of the River Iberus, flowing southeast into the Mediterranean Sea. Its name, Iberus, has gradually changed, in modern times, to Ebro. By the treaty with the Romans, the Carthaginians were not to cross the Iberus. They were also bound by the treaty not to interfere with the people of Saguntum, a city lying between the Iberus and the Carthaginian dominions. Saguntum was in alliance with the Romans and under their protection.

Hamilcar was, however, very restless and uneasy at being required to refrain from hostilities with the Roman power. He began, immediately after his arrival in Spain, to form plans for renewing the war. He had under him, as his principal lieutenant, a young man who had married his daughter. His name was Hasdrubal. With Hasdrubal's aid Hamilcar went on extending his conquests in Spain, strengthening his position there and gradually maturing his plans for renewing war with the Romans, when after some time he died. Hasdrubal succeeded him. Hannibal was probably about twenty-one or -two years old and still in Carthage. Hasdrubal sent to the Carthaginian government a request that Hannibal might receive an appointment in the army and be sent out to join him in Spain.

There was a great debate in the Carthaginian senate on the subject of complying with this request. In all cases where questions of government are controlled by votes, it has been found, in every age, that parties will always be formed, of which the two most prominent will usually be nearly balanced one against the other. At the time, the Hamilcar family was in power; however, there was a strong party in Carthage in opposition to them. The leader of the party in the senate, whose name was Hanno, made a very earnest speech against sending Hannibal. He was too young, he said, to be of any service. He would only learn the vices and follies of the camp and thus become corrupted and ruined. "Besides," said Hanno, "at this rate, the command of our armies in Spain is getting to be a sort of hereditary right. Hamilcar was not a king. Why should his authority descend first to his son-in-law and then to his son? This plan of making Hannibal, while yet scarcely arrived at manhood, a high officer in the army is only a stepping-stone to putting the forces totally under his command, when, for any reason, Hasdrubal ceases to command them."

The Roman historian, whose narrative gives us our only account of this debate, says that, though these were good reasons, strength prevailed over wisdom in the decision. They voted to send Hannibal, and he set out to cross the sea to Spain with a heart full of enthusiasm and joy.

A great deal of curiosity and interest was felt throughout the army to see him on his arrival. The soldiers had been devotedly attached to his father, and they were all ready to transfer this attachment at once to the son, if he should prove worthy of it. It was evident, soon after he reached the camp that he was going to prove himself worthy. He entered immediately into the duties of his position with a degree of energy, patience, and self-denial which attracted the attention of all and made him a favorite. He dressed plainly; he assumed no airs; he sought no pleasures or indulgences nor demanded any exemption from the dangers and lack of basic necessities which the common soldiers had to endure. He ate plain food and slept, often in his military cloak, on the ground, in the midst of the soldiers on guard; and in battle he was always the first to press forward into the contest and the last to leave the ground when the time came for rest. The Romans say that, in addition to these qualities, he was inhuman and merciless when in open warfare with his foes, and cunning and treacherous in every other method of dealing with them. Such traits of character were considered by soldiers in those days, as they are now, virtues in themselves, though vices in their enemies.

However, Hannibal became a great favorite in the army. He went on for several years increasing his military knowledge and widening and extending his influence, when one day, Hasdrubal was suddenly killed by a ferocious native of Spain whom he had in some way offended. As soon as the first shock of the news was over, the leaders of the army went in pursuit of Hannibal, whom they brought in triumph to the tent of Hasdrubal, and instated him at once in the supreme command, with one consent and in the midst of universal acclamations. As soon as news of this event reached Carthage, the government there confirmed the act of the army, and Hannibal found himself suddenly but securely invested with a very high military command.

His eager and restless desire to try his strength with the Romans received a new motivation by his finding that the power was now in his hands. Still the two countries were at peace, and they were bound by solemn treaties to continue to keep the peace. The River Iberus was the boundary which separated the dominions of the two nations from each other in Spain, the territory east of that boundary being under the Roman power and that on the west under the Carthaginians; except that Saguntum, which was on the western side, was an ally of the Romans, and the Carthaginians were bound by the treaty to leave it independent and free.

Hannibal could not, therefore, cross the Iberus or attack Saguntum without an open infraction of the treaty. However, he immediately began to move toward Saguntum to attack the nations in the immediate vicinity of it. If he wished to get into a war with the Romans, this was the proper way to promote it; for by advancing into the immediate vicinity of the capital of their allies, there was great probability that disputes would arise which would sooner or later provoke war.

The Romans say that Hannibal was cunning and treacherous, and he certainly did display, on some occasions, a great degree of genius in his maneuvers. In one instance in these preliminary wars, he gained a victory over an

immensely superior force in a very remarkable manner.
He was returning from an invasion on some of the northern provinces, laden and encumbered with spoil, when he
learned that an immense army, consisting, it was said, of a
hundred thousand men, was coming up from behind him.
There was a river a short distance in front of him. Hannibal pressed on and crossed the river by a stream, the water
being, perhaps, about three feet deep. He concealed a large
body of cavalry near the bank of the stream and pushed on
with the main body of the army to a short distance from
the river, so as to produce the impression on his pursuers
that he was pressing forward to make his escape.

The enemy, thinking that they had no time to lose,
poured down in great numbers into the stream from various
points along the banks; and as soon as they had reached the
middle of the current and were wading laboriously, half-
submerged, with their weapons held above their heads, in
order to present as little resistance as possible to the water,
the horsemen of Hannibal rushed in to meet and attack
them. The horsemen had, of course, the greater advantage; for though their horses were in the water, they were
themselves raised above it, and their limbs were free, while
their enemies, half-submerged and burdened by their weapons and by one another, were nearly helpless. They were
immediately thrown into complete confusion and were
overwhelmed and carried down by the current in great
numbers. Some of them succeeded in landing below, on
Hannibal's side; but, in the meantime, the main body of his
army had returned and was ready to receive them, and they
were trampled under foot by the elephants, which it was
the custom to employ, in those days, as a military force. As
soon as the river was cleared, Hannibal marched his own
army across it and attacked what remained of the enemy

on their own side. He gained a complete victory, which was so great and decisive that he secured by it possession of the whole country west of the Iberus, except Saguntum, and Saguntum itself began to be seriously alarmed.

The Saguntines sent ambassadors to Rome to ask the Romans to intervene and protect them from the dangers which threatened them. The ambassadors made diligent efforts to reach Rome as soon as possible, but they were too late. On some pretext or other, Hannibal devised a plan to raise a dispute between the city and one of the neighboring tribes, and then, taking sides with the tribe, he advanced to attack the city. The Saguntines prepared for their defense, hoping soon to receive assistance in their time of distress from Rome. They strengthened and fortified their walls, while Hannibal began to move forward great military engines for battering them down.

Hannibal knew very well that by his hostilities against this city he was commencing a contest with Rome itself, as Rome must take part with her ally. In fact, there is no doubt that his plan was to bring on a general war between the two great nations. He began with Saguntum for two reasons: first, it would not be safe for him to cross the Iberus and advance into the Roman territory, leaving so wealthy and powerful a city in his rear; and in the second place, it was easier for him to find reasons for getting indirectly into a quarrel with Saguntum and throwing the provocation of a declaration of war on Rome than to persuade the Carthaginian state to renounce the peace and themselves commence hostilities. There was, as has been already stated, a very strong party at Carthage opposed to Hannibal, who would, of course, resist any measures leading to a war with Rome, for they would consider such a war as opening a vast field for gratifying Hannibal's

ambition. The only way, therefore, was to provoke a war
by aggressions on the Roman allies and to justify it with
the best reasons he could find.

Saguntum was a very wealthy and powerful city. It
was situated about a mile from the sea. The attack on the
place, and the defense of it by the inhabitants, went on for
some time with great vigor. In these operations, Hannibal
exposed himself to great danger. He approached, at one
time, so near the wall, in superintending the arrangements
of his soldiers and the planting of his engines, that a heavy
javelin, thrown from the parapet, struck him on the thigh.
It pierced the flesh and inflicted so severe a wound that
he fell immediately and was carried away by the soldiers.
It was several days before he was free from the danger
incurred by the loss of blood and the fever which follows
such a wound. During all this time his army was in a great
state of anxiety and suspended their active operations. As
soon as Hannibal was found to be healthy, they resumed
their operations again and he urged them onward with
greater energy than before.

The weapons of warfare in those ancient days were
entirely different from those which are now employed, and
there was one, described by an ancient historian as used
by the Saguntines at this siege, which might almost come
under the modern definition of firearms. It was called the
falarica. It was a sort of javelin, consisting of a shaft of
wood with a long point of iron. This point was said to be
three feet long. This javelin was to be thrown at the enemy
either from the hand of the soldier or by an engine. The
most peculiar thing about it was that, near the pointed end,
long bands of fiber were wound around the wooden shaft.
These were saturated with pitch and other combustibles,
and this flammable band was set on fire just before the

javelin was thrown. As the missile flew on its way, the wind fanned the flames and made them burn so fiercely that when the javelin struck the shield of the soldier opposing it, it could not be pulled out, and the shield itself had to be thrown down and abandoned.

While the inhabitants of Saguntum were vainly trying to defend themselves against their terrible enemy by these and similar means, their ambassadors, not knowing that the city had been attacked, had reached Rome and had laid before the Roman senate their fears that the city would be attacked, unless they adopted vigorous and immediate measures to prevent it. The Romans resolved to send ambassadors to Hannibal to demand of him what his intentions were and to warn him against any acts of hostility against Saguntum. When these Roman ambassadors arrived on the coast, near to Saguntum, they found that hostilities had commenced and that the city was hotly besieged. They were at a loss to know what to do.

Hannibal, with clever skillfulness which the Carthaginians called sagacity, and the Romans call treachery and cunning, made every effort to avoid the ambassadors. He sent word to them, at the shore, that they must not attempt to come to his camp, for the country was in such a disturbed condition that it would not be safe for them to land; and besides, he could not receive or attend to them, for he was too much pressed with the urgency of his military works to have anytime to spare for debates and negotiations.

Hannibal knew that the ambassadors, being rejected and having found that the war had broken out and that Saguntum had actually been attacked and besieged by Hannibal's armies, would proceed immediately to Carthage to demand satisfaction there. He also knew that Hanno and his party would very probably adopt the cause of the Romans

and attempt to stop his plans. So he sent his own ambassadors to Carthage, to exert an influence in his favor in the
Carthaginian senate and attempt to urge them to reject the
claims of the Romans and allow the war between Rome
and Carthage to break out again.

The Roman ambassadors appeared at Carthage and
were admitted to an audience before the senate. They stated
their case, representing that Hannibal had made war upon
Saguntum in violation of the treaty and had refused even
to receive the communication which had been sent him
by the Roman senate through them. They demanded that
the Carthaginian government condemn his acts and deliver
him up to them, in order that he might receive the punishment which his violation of the treaty and his aggressions
on an ally of the Romans so justly deserved.

The party of Hannibal in the Carthaginian senate was,
of course, eager to have these proposals rejected with scorn.
The other side, with Hanno at their head, maintained that
they were reasonable demands. Hanno, in a very energetic
and powerful speech, told the senate that he had warned
them not to send Hannibal into Spain. He had foreseen
that such a hot and turbulent spirit as his would involve
them in inextricable difficulties with the Roman power.
Hannibal had, he said, plainly violated the treaty. He had
attacked and besieged Saguntum, with whom they were
solemnly bound not to intervene, and they had nothing to
expect in return but that the Roman legions would soon
be attacking and besieging their own city. In the meantime,
he added, the Romans, had been moderate and forbearing.
They had brought nothing to the charge of the Carthaginians. They accused nobody but Hannibal, who, thus far,
alone was guilty. The Carthaginians, by condemning his
acts, could save themselves from the responsibility of them.

He urged, therefore, that a message of apology should be sent to Rome, that Hannibal should be removed from his command and delivered up to the Romans, and that ample restitution should be made to the Saguntines for the injuries they had received.

On the other hand, the friends of Hannibal defended the actions of their general to the Carthaginian senate. They reviewed the history of the transactions in which the war had originated and showed, or attempted to show, that the Saguntines themselves commenced hostilities. Consequently, they, and not Hannibal, were responsible for all that followed; that, under those circumstances, the Romans ought not to take their part, and if they did so, it proved that they preferred the friendship of Saguntum to that of Carthage; and that it would be extremely cowardly and dishonorable for the Carthaginians to deliver the general whom they had placed in power, and who had shown himself so worthy of their choice by his courage and energy, into the hands of their ancient and merciless foes.

Therefore, Hannibal was waging two wars at the same time, one in the Carthaginian senate, where the weapons were arguments and eloquence, and the other under the walls of Saguntum, which was fought with battering rams and fiery javelins. He conquered in both. The senate decided to send the Roman ambassadors home without agreeing to their demands, and the walls of Saguntum were battered down by Hannibal's engines. The inhabitants refused all terms of compromise and resisted to the last, so that, when the victorious soldiers broke over the flattened walls and poured into the city, it was given up to them to plunder, and they killed and destroyed all that came in their way. The disappointed ambassadors returned to Rome with the news that Saguntum had been taken and destroyed by

Hannibal and that the Carthaginians, far from offering any satisfaction for the wrong, assumed the responsibility of it themselves and were preparing for war.

Thus Hannibal accomplished his purpose of opening the way for waging war against the Roman power. He prepared to enter into the contest with the utmost energy and zeal. The conflict that ensued lasted seventeen years and is known in history as the second Punic war. It was one of the most dreadful struggles between rival and hostile nations which the gloomy history of mankind exhibits to view. The events that occurred will be described in the subsequent chapters.

CHAPTER III

OPENING OF THE
SECOND PUNIC WAR.

NCE the tide turns in favor of any nation in war, it generally rushes on with great haste and force and bears all before it. So it was in Carthage. The party of Hanno was thrown entirely into the minority and silenced, and the friends and partisans of Hannibal carried not only the government, but the whole community with them, and everybody was eager for war. This was due, in part, to the natural contagiousness of the warlike spirit, which, when felt by one, easily catches sympathy in the heart of another. It is a fire which, once it begins to burn, spreads in every direction and consumes all that comes in its way.

When Hannibal gained possession of Saguntum, he found immense treasures there, which he took, not to increase his own private fortune but to strengthen and confirm his civil and military power. The Saguntines did everything they could to prevent these treasures from falling into his hands. They fought desperately to the last and refused all terms of surrender. They became so insanely desperate in the end, that when they found that the walls and towers of the city were falling in and that all hope of further defense was gone, they built an enormous fire in the public streets and heaped on it all the treasures that fire could destroy, and then many of the principal inhabitants leaped into the flames, in order that their hated conquerors might lose their prisoners as well as their spoils.

Notwithstanding this, however, Hannibal obtained a vast amount of gold and silver, and also much valuable merchandise, which the Saguntine merchants had accumulated in their palaces and warehouses. He paid his soldiers all the back pay due in full. He divided amongst them a large additional amount as their share of the spoil. He sent rich trophies home to Carthage and presents, consisting of sums of money, jewelry, and gems, to his friends there and to those whom he wished to make his friends. The result of this great generosity, and of the widespread fame which his victories in Spain had brought, was to raise him to the highest pinnacle of influence and honor. The Carthaginians chose to make him one of the *suffetes*.

The suffetes were the supreme executive officers of the Carthaginian commonwealth. The government was, as has been remarked before, a sort of aristocratic republic, and republics are always very cautious about entrusting power, even executive power, to any one man. As Rome had two consuls, reigning jointly, and France, after her first revolution, a Directory of five, so the Carthaginians chose annually two suffetes, as they were called at Carthage, though the Roman writers indiscriminately call them suffetes, consuls, and kings. In conjunction with his colleague, Hannibal held the supreme civil authority in Carthage. Additionally, Hannibal was in command of the vast and victorious army in Spain.

When news of these events—the siege and destruction of Saguntum, the rejection of the demands of the Roman ambassadors, and the vigorous preparations made by the Carthaginians for war—reached Rome, the whole city was thrown into terror. The senate and the people held disorderly assemblies, in which these events and the course Rome should take were discussed with much excitement and clamor. The Romans were, in fact, afraid of the Carthaginians. The military operations of Hannibal in Spain had left the people with a strong sense of the relentless and terrible energy of his character. They at once concluded that his plans would be to march into Italy, and they anticipated the danger of his bringing the war up to the very gates of the city, so as to threaten them with the destruction which he had brought upon Saguntum. This conclusion showed how much they were aware of his character.

Since the conclusion of the first Punic war, there had been peace between the Romans and Carthaginians for about a quarter of a century. During all this time both nations had advanced in wealth and power, but the Carthaginians had made much more rapid progress than the Romans. The Romans had, indeed, been very successful at the outset in the former war, but in the end the Carthaginians had proved themselves their equal. They seemed, therefore, to dread a fresh encounter with these powerful foes, led on by such a commander as Hannibal.

They made plans, therefore, to send a second delegation to Carthage, with a view of making one more effort to preserve peace before actually commencing hostilities. They selected five men from among the most influential citizens of the state—older men of impressive dignity and of great public consideration—and commissioned them to proceed to Carthage and ask once more whether it was the deliberate and final decision of the Carthaginian senate to

openly declare and support the actions of Hannibal. This
solemn delegation set sail. They arrived at Carthage. They
appeared before the senate. They argued their cause, but it
was, of course, to deaf and unwilling ears. The Carthaginian orators replied to them, each side attempting to throw
the blame of the violation of the treaty on the other. It
was a solemn hour, for the peace of the world, the lives of
hundreds of thousands of people, and the continued happiness or the desolation and ruin of vast regions of country
depended on the result of the debate.

Unhappily, the breach was only widened by the discussion. "Very well," said the Roman commissioners, at
last, "we offer you peace or war, which do you choose?"
"Whichever you please," replied the Carthaginians; "decide
for yourselves." "War, then," said the Romans, "since it
must be so." The conference was broken up, and the ambassadors returned to Rome.

They returned, however, by way of Spain. Their object
in doing this was to negotiate with the various kingdoms
and tribes in Spain and in France, through which Hannibal
would have to march in invading Italy, and endeavor to
induce them to take sides with the Romans. They were too
late, however, for Hannibal had already managed to extend
and establish his influence in all that region too strongly
to be shaken; so that, on one pretext or another, the Roman proposals were all rejected. There was one powerful
tribe, for example, called the Volscians. The ambassadors,
in the presence of the great council of the Volscians, made
known to them the probability of war and invited them to
align themselves with the Romans. The Volscians rejected
the proposition with a sort of scorn. "We see," said they,
"from the fate of Saguntum, what is to be expected to
result from an alliance with the Romans. After leaving

that city defenseless and alone in its struggle against such
terrible danger, it is in vain to ask other nations to trust to
your protection. If you wish for new allies, it will be best
for you to go where the story of Saguntum is not known."
This answer of the Volscians was applauded by the other
nations of Spain, as far as it was known, and the Roman
ambassadors, with no hope of success in that country, went
on into Gaul, which is the name France was known by in
ancient history.

On reaching a certain place which was a central point
of influence and power in Gaul, the Roman commissioners convened a great warlike council. The spectacle presented by this assembly was very imposing, for the warlike
counselors came to the meeting armed completely and in
the most formidable manner, as if they were coming to a
battle instead of a consultation and debate. The venerable
ambassadors laid the subject before them. They concentrated their discussion largely on the power and greatness
of the Romans and on the certainty that they should conquer in the approaching operations, and they invited the
Gauls to adopt their cause and to rise in arms and intercept
Hannibal's passage through their country, if he should attempt to make one.

The assembly could hardly be induced to hear the ambassadors through, and as soon as they had finished their
address, the whole council broke forth into cries of dissent
and displeasure, and even into shouts of derision. Order
was eventually restored, and the officers, whose duty it
was to express the sentiments of the assembly, gave for
their reply that the Gauls had never received anything but
violence and injuries from Rome or anything but kindness
and goodwill from Carthage. They had no thoughts of being guilty of the folly of bringing the impending storm

of Hannibal's hostility upon their own heads, merely for the sake of averting it from their ancient and implacable foes. Thus the ambassadors were denied everywhere. They found no friendship toward the Roman power until they crossed the Rhone.

In a very deliberate and cautious manner, Hannibal began to form his plans for a march into Italy. He knew well that it was an expedition of such magnitude and duration as to require beforehand the most careful and well-considered arrangements, both for the forces which were to go and for the states and communities which were to remain. The winter was coming on. His first act was to dismiss a large portion of his forces that they might visit their homes. He told them that he was intending some great plans for the coming spring, which might take them to a great distance and keep them for a long time absent from Spain, and he would, accordingly, give them the intervening time to visit their families and their homes and to arrange their affairs. This act of kind consideration and confidence renewed the attachment of the soldiers to their commander, and they returned to his camp in the spring not only with new strength and vigor but with redoubled attachment to the service in which they were engaged.

Hannibal, after sending his soldiers home, withdrew to New Carthage, which is farther west than Saguntum, where he went into winter quarters and devoted himself to the maturing of his plans. Besides the necessary preparations for his own march, he had to provide for the government of the countries that he should leave. He devised various and ingenious plans to prevent the danger of revolts and rebellions while he was gone. One was to organize an army for Spain out of soldiers drawn from Africa, while the troops which were to be employed to protect Carthage and to sustain the government there were taken from Spain. By changing the troops of the two countries, each country was controlled by foreign troops, who were more likely to be faithful in their obedience to their commanders and less in danger of sympathizing with the populations which they were respectively employed to control than if each had been retained in its own native land.

Hannibal knew very well that the various states and provinces of Spain, which had refused to align themselves with the Romans and abandon him, had been led to do this through the influence of his presents or the fear of his power. If after he penetrated into Italy he should meet with a change of this condition, so as to diminish their hope of deriving benefit from his favor or their fear of his power, he knew there would be great danger of defections and revolts. As an additional security against this, he adopted the following ingenious plan. He enlisted a body of troops from among all the nations of Spain that were in alliance with him, selecting young men who were from families of consideration and influence, and this body of troops, when organized and officered, was sent into Carthage, giving the nations and tribes from which they were drawn to understand that he considered them not only as soldiers serving in his armies, but as hostages, which he should hold as security for the fidelity and obedience of the countries from which they had come. The number of these soldiers was four thousand.

Hannibal had a brother, whose name, as it happened, was the same as that of his brother-in-law, Hasdrubal. It was to him that he committed the government of Spain during his absence. The soldiers provided for him were, as has been already stated, mainly drawn from Africa. In addition to the foot soldiers, he provided him with a small body of horsemen. He left with him, also, fourteen elephants. And as he thought it possible that the Romans might, in some contingency during his absence, make a descent upon the Spanish coast from the sea, he built and equipped for Hasdrubal a small fleet of about sixty vessels, fifty of which were of the first class. In modern times, the magnitude and efficiency of a ship is estimated by the number of guns she will carry; then it was the number of banks of oars. Fifty of Hasdrubal's ships were *quinqueremes*— they had five banks of oars.

The Romans, on the other hand, did not neglect their own preparations. Though reluctant to enter into war, when they found that it could not be averted, they still prepared to engage in it with their characteristic energy and enthusiasm,. They raised two powerful armies, one for each of the consuls. The plan was for one of these to advance to meet Hannibal and for the other to proceed to Sicily and from Sicily to the African coast, with a view of threatening the Carthaginian capital. This plan, if successful, would compel the Carthaginians to recall a part or the whole of Hannibal's army from the intended invasion of Italy to defend their own African homes.

The force raised by the Romans amounted to about seventy thousand men. About a third of these were Roman soldiers, and the remainder were drawn from various nations dwelling in Italy and in the islands of the Mediterranean Sea which were in alliance with the Romans. Of these troops six thousand were cavalry. Of course, as the Romans intended to cross into Africa, they needed a fleet. They built and equipped one, which consisted of two hundred and twenty ships of the largest class, that is, quinqueremes, and a number of smaller and lighter vessels for services requiring speed. There were vessels in use in those times larger than the quinqueremes. Mention is occasionally made of those which had six and even seven banks of oars. But these were only employed as the flagships of commanders and for other purposes of ceremony and parade, as they were too unwieldy for efficient service in action.

Lots were then drawn in a very solemn manner, according to the Roman custom on such occasions, to decide on the assignment of these two armies to the respective consuls. The one destined to meet Hannibal on his way from Spain fell to a consul named Cornelius Scipio. The name of the other was Sempronius. It fell to him, consequently, to take charge of the expedition destined for Sicily and Africa. When all the arrangements were made, the question was finally put, in a very solemn and formal manner, to the Roman people for their final vote and decision. "Do the Roman people decide and decree that war shall be declared against the Carthaginians?" The decision was in the affirmative. The war was then proclaimed with the usual impressive ceremonies. Sacrifices and religious celebrations followed to satisfy the wrath and win the favor of the gods and to inspire the soldiers with that kind of courage and confidence which the superstitious, however wicked, feel when they can imagine themselves under the protection of heaven. When the shows and displays were over, all things were ready.

In the meantime Hannibal was moving on, as the spring advanced, toward the banks of the Iberus, that frontier stream, the crossing of which made him an invader of what was, in some sense, Roman territory. He boldly passed the stream and moved forward along the coast of the Mediterranean, gradually approaching the Pyrenees, mountains which form the boundary between France and Spain. His soldiers up to this time did not know what his plans were. It is rarely the custom now for military and naval commanders to communicate to their men much information about their plans, and it was still less the custom then; also, in those days, the common soldiers had no access to those means of information by which news of every sort is now so universally diffused. And so, though all the officers of the army and well-informed citizens both in Rome and Carthage anticipated and understood Hannibal's plans, his own ignorant soldiers knew nothing except that they were to go on some distant and dangerous service. They very likely had no idea whatever of Italy or of Rome or of the magnitude of the possessions or of the power held by the vast empire which they were going to invade.

When, however, after traveling day after day, they came to the foot of the Pyrenees and found that they were really going to pass that mighty chain of mountains and for this purpose were actually entering its wild and gloomy passes, the courage of some of them failed and they began to murmur. The discontent and alarm were, in fact, so great that one corps, consisting of about three thousand men, left the camp in a body and moved back toward their homes. On inquiry, Hannibal found that there were ten thousand more who were in a similar state of feeling. His whole force consisted of over one hundred thousand. What do you imagine Hannibal would do in such an emergency? Would he return in pursuit of the deserters to recapture and destroy them as a terror to the rest? Or would he let them go and attempt by words to overcome their distrust and encourage them to confirm and save those that yet remained? He did neither. He called together the ten thousand discontented troops that were still in his camp and told them that, since they were afraid to accompany his army or unwilling to do so, they might as well return home. He wanted none in his service who had not the courage and fortitude to go on wherever he might lead. He would not have the fainthearted and the timid in his army. They would only be a burden to weigh down and impede the courage and energy of the rest. So saying, he gave orders for them to return, and with the rest of the army, whose resolution and fervor were redoubled by this action, he moved on through the passes of the mountains.

This act of Hannibal, in permitting his discontented soldiers to return, had all the effect of a deed of generosity in its influence upon the minds of the soldiers who went on. We must not, however, imagine that it was prompted by a spirit of generosity at all. A seeming generosity was, in this case, exactly what was wanted to answer his ends. Hannibal was mercilessly cruel in all cases where he imagined that severity was demanded. It requires great discernment sometimes in a commander to know when he must punish and when it is wisest to overlook and forgive. Hannibal, like Alexander and Napoleon, possessed this discernment in a very high degree; and it was, doubtless, the exercise of that principle alone which prompted his action on this occasion.

Thus Hannibal passed the Pyrenees. The next difficulty he anticipated was crossing the River Rhone.

CHAPTER IV

THE PASSAGE OF THE RHONE.

ANNIBAL, after he had passed the Pyrenees, did not anticipate any new difficulties until he arrived at the Rhone. He knew very well it was a broad and rapid river and that he must cross it near its mouth, where the water was deep and the banks low. Besides, it was possible that the Romans who were coming to meet him, under Cornelius Scipio, might reach the Rhone before he could arrive there and be ready upon the banks to block his passage. He sent forward, therefore, a small detachment in advance to make a preliminary survey of the country and select a route to the Rhone, and if they met with no difficulties to stop them there, they were to go on until they reached the Alps and explore the passes through which his army could best cross those snow-covered mountains.

It seems that before he reached the Pyrenees—that is, while he was upon the Spanish side of them—some of the tribes through whose territories he had to pass undertook

to resist him, and he had to attack them and reduce them
by force. Then, when he was ready to move on, he left a
guard in the territories which he had conquered to keep
them in subjection. Rumors of this reached Gaul. The
Gauls were alarmed for their own safety. They had not
intended to oppose Hannibal so long as they supposed
that he only wished for a safe passage through their country on his way to Italy; but now, when they found, from
what had occurred in Spain, that he was going to conquer
the countries he moved through as he passed along, they
became alarmed. They seized their arms and assembled
in haste at Ruscino and began to plan for their defense.
Ruscino was the same place that the Roman ambassadors
met the great council of the Gauls on their return to Italy
from Carthage.

While the assembly of armies was gathering at Ruscino,
full of threats and anger, Hannibal was at Illiberis, a town
at the foot of the Pyrenean Mountains. It appeared he had
no fear that any opposition which the Gauls could bring
to bear against him would be successful, but he dreaded
the delay. He was extremely unwilling to spend the precious months of the early summer contending with such
foes as they, when the road to Italy was before him. Besides, the passes of the Alps, which are difficult and require
extreme care at anytime, are utterly impassable except in
the months of July and August. At all other seasons they
are, or were in those days, blocked up with heavy snows.
In modern times roads have been made, with tunnels cut
through the rock and with the exposed places protected
by sloping roofs projecting from above, over which storms
sweep and avalanches slide without causing injury; so that
now ordinary travel between France and Italy, across the
Alps continues, in some measure, all year. However, in

Hannibal's time, the mountains could not be traveled except in the summer months. Had the result not justified the undertaking, it would have been considered an act of inexcusable rashness and folly to attempt to cross with an army at all.

Hannibal had no time to lose and that circumstance made this case one of those in which indulgence and a show of generosity were called for, instead of defiance and force. He accordingly sent messengers to the council at Ruscino to say, in a very gracious and courteous manner, that he wished to see and confer with their princes in person and that, if they pleased, he would advance for this purpose toward Ruscino; or they might, if they preferred, come toward him at Illiberis, where he would await their arrival. He invited them to come freely into his camp and said that he was ready, if they were willing to receive him, to go into theirs, for he had come to Gaul as a friend and an ally and wanted nothing but a free passage through their territory. He had made a resolution, he said, if the Gauls would but allow him to keep it, that there should not be a single sword drawn in his army until he got into Italy.

The alarm and the feelings of hostility which prevailed among the Gauls were greatly lessened by this message. They put their camp in motion and went on to Illiberis. The princes and high officers of their armies went to Hannibal's camp and were received with the highest marks of distinction and honor. They were loaded with presents and went away charmed with the friendliness, the wealth, and the generosity of their visitor. Instead of opposing his progress, they became the conductors and guides of his army. They took them first to Ruscino, their capital, and then, after a short delay, the army moved on without any further interference toward the Rhone.

In the meantime, the Roman consul Scipio, having boarded the troops destined to meet Hannibal in sixty ships at the mouth of the Tiber, set sail for the mouth of the Rhone. The men were crowded together in the ships, as armies necessarily must be when transported by sea. They could not go far out to sea, for, as they had no compass in those days, there were no means of directing the course of navigation, in case of storms or cloudy skies, except by the land. The ships made their way slowly along the shore, sometimes by means of sails and sometimes by oars, and after suffering for sometime the hardships and lack of basic necessities natural to such a voyage—the sea sickness and the confinement of such swarming numbers in so narrow a space bringing every kind of discomfort—the fleet entered the mouth of the Rhone. The officers had no idea that Hannibal was near. They had only heard of his having crossed the Iberus. They imagined that he was still on the other side of the Pyrenees. They entered the Rhone by the first branch they came to—for the Rhone, like the Nile, divides near its mouth and flows into the sea by several separate channels—and sailed without concern up to Marseilles, imagining that their enemy was still hundreds of miles away, entangled, perhaps, among the passes of the Pyrenees. Instead, he was safely camped upon the banks of the Rhone, a short distance above them, quietly and coolly making his arrangements for crossing it.

When Cornelius got his men on land, they were too much exhausted by the sickness and misery they had endured on the voyage to move on to meet Hannibal without some days for rest and refreshment. Cornelius, however, selected three hundred horsemen who were able to move and sent them up the river on an exploring expedition to learn the facts in respect to Hannibal and to report them to him. Dispatching them, he remained in the camp, reorganizing and recruiting his army and awaiting the return of the party that he had sent to explore.

Although Hannibal had met with no serious opposition in his progress through Gaul, it must not, on that account, be supposed that the people, through whose territories he was passing, were friendly to his cause or pleased with his presence among them. An army is always a burden and a curse to any country that it enters, even when its only object is to pass through peacefully. The Gauls assumed a friendly attitude toward this dreaded invader and his horde only because they thought that by so doing he would the sooner pass and be gone. They were too weak and had too few means of resistance to attempt to stop him; and, as the next best thing that they could do, they resolved to give him every possible aid to hasten him on his way. This continued to be the policy of the various tribes until he reached the river. The people on the other side of the river, however, thought it was best to resist. They were nearer to the Roman territories and, consequently, somewhat more under Roman influence. They feared the resentment of the Romans if they should, even passively, render any cooperation to Hannibal in his plans; and as they had the broad and rapid river between them and their enemy, they thought there was a reasonable chance that, with its aid, they could exclude him from their territories altogether.

Consequently, when Hannibal came to the stream, the people on one side were all eager to help, while those on the other were determined to prevent his passage, both parties being filled by the same desire to free their country from such a pest as the presence of an army of ninety thousand men. When Hannibal stood at last on the banks of the river, the people on his side of the stream were waiting and ready to furnish all the boats and vessels that they could command and to give every aid in their power for his departure. Those on the other side were drawn up in battle lines, rank behind rank, glittering with weapons, arranged so as to guard every place of landing, and lining with pikes the whole extent of the shore, while the peaks of their tents, in vast numbers, with banners among them floating in the air, were to be seen in the distance behind them. All this time the three hundred horsemen which Cornelius had dispatched were slowly and cautiously making their way up the river from the Roman camp below.

After contemplating the scene presented to his view at the river for sometime in silence, Hannibal began his preparations for crossing the stream. He collected first all the boats of every kind which could be obtained among the Gauls who lived along the bank of the river. These, however, only served for a beginning, and so he next got together all the workmen and all the tools which the country could furnish, for several miles around, and went to work constructing more. The Gauls of that region had a custom of making boats from the trunks of large trees. The tree, being cut down then cut to the proper length, was hollowed out with hatchets and axes, and then, being turned bottom upward, the outside was shaped in such a manner as to make it glide easily through the water. So convenient is this mode of making boats that it is practiced, in cases where sufficiently large trees are found, to the present day. Such boats are called canoes.

There were plenty of large trees on the banks of the Rhone. Hannibal's soldiers watched the Gauls at their work making boats of them, until they learned the art themselves. Some first assisted their new allies in the easier portions of the operation and then began to fell large trees and make the boats themselves. Others, who had less skill or were more impetuous chose not to wait for the slow process of hollowing the wood. They would cut down the trees on the shore, cut the trunks of equal lengths, place them side by side in the water, and bolt or bind them together so as to form a raft. The form and fashion of their craft was not important, they said, as it was for one passage only. Anything would meet their need if it would only float and bear its burden over.

In the meantime, the enemy on the opposite shore looked on, but they could do nothing to impede these operations. If they'd had artillery like our present day armies, they could have fired across the river and blown the boats and rafts to pieces with balls and shells as fast as the Gauls and Carthaginians could build them. In fact, the workmen could not have built them under such an attack; but the enemy, in this case, had nothing but spears and arrows and stones, to be thrown either by the hand or by engines far too weak to send them with any effect across such a river. They had to look on quietly, therefore, and allow these great and formidable preparations for an attack upon them to go on without interruption. Their only hope was to overwhelm the army with their missiles and prevent their landing, when they should reach the bank at last in their attempt to cross the stream.

If an army is crossing a river without any enemy to oppose them, a moderate number of boats will serve, since smaller groups of the army can be transported at a time, and the whole army gradually transferred from one bank to the other by repeated trips. But when there is an enemy to encounter at the landing, it is necessary to provide the means of carrying over a very large force all at once; for if a small division were to go over alone, it would only throw itself, weak and defenseless, into the hands of the enemy. Hannibal, therefore, waited until he had boats, rafts, and floats enough constructed to carry over a force sufficiently numerous and powerful to attack the enemy with a good chance of success.

The Romans, as we have already remarked, say that Hannibal was cunning. He certainly was not inclined, like Alexander, to trust his battles to simple superiority of bravery and force but was always coming up with some plan to increase the chances of victory. He did so in this case. He kept up for many days a parade and energy of building boats and rafts in sight of his enemy, as if his sole reliance was on the multitude of men that he could pour across the river at a single transportation, and he thus kept their attention closely riveted upon these preparations. All this time, however, he had another plan already in action. He had sent a strong body of troops secretly up the river, with orders to make their way quietly through the forests and cross the stream some few miles above. This force was intended to move back from the river, as soon as it should cross the stream and come down upon the enemy in the rear, so as to attack them there at the same time that Hannibal was crossing with the main body of the army. If they succeeded in crossing the river safely, they were to build a fire in the woods, on the other side, in order that the column of smoke which should ascend from it might serve as a signal of their success to Hannibal.

This detachment was commanded by an officer named Hanno—of course a very different man from Hannibal's great enemy of that name in Carthage. Hanno set out in the night, moving back from the river, in beginning his march, so as to be entirely out of sight from the Gauls on the other side. He had some guides, belonging to the country, who promised to show him a convenient place for crossing. The party went up the river about twenty-five miles. Here they found a place where the water spread to a greater width, the current was less rapid and the water not so deep. They got to this place in silence and secrecy, their enemies below not having suspected any such design. As they had nobody to oppose them, they could cross much more easily than the main army below. They made some rafts for carrying over the men that could not swim, and such weapons and ammunition that would be damaged by the water. The rest of the men waded until they reached the channel and then swam, supporting themselves in part by their bucklers, which they placed beneath their bodies in the water. Thus they all crossed in safety. They paused a day to dry their clothes and to rest and then moved cautiously down the river until they were near enough to Hannibal's position to allow their signal to be seen. The fire was then built, and they gazed with triumphant joy upon the column of smoke which ascended from it high into the air.

Hannibal saw the signal and now immediately pre-pared to cross with his army. The horsemen embarked in boats, holding their horses by lines, with a view of leading them into the water so that they might swim in company with the boats. Other bridled horses were put into large flat-bottomed boats to be taken across dry, in order that they might be all ready for service at the instant of land-ing. The most vigorous and efficient portion of the army was, of course, selected for the first passage, while all those who, for any cause, were weak or disabled, remained be-hind, with the stores and weapons and ammunitions of war, to be transported afterward, when the first passage was successful. All this time the enemy, on the opposite shore, was getting its ranks in line and making everything ready for a furious assault upon the invaders the moment they should approach the land.

There was something like silence and order during the period while the men were embarking and pushing out from the land, but as they advanced into the current, the loud commands and shouts and outcries increased more and more, and the quickness of the current and of the whirlpools by which the boats and rafts were hurried down the stream soon produced a terrific scene of commotion and confusion. As soon as the first boats approached the land, the Gauls assembled to oppose them rushed down upon them with showers of missiles and with those unearthly yells which barbarous warriors always raise in going into battle, as a means both of exciting themselves and of terrifying their enemy. Hannibal's officers urged the boats on and made an earnest attempt, with as much coolness and deliberation as possible, to secure a landing. It is perhaps doubtful how the contest would have ended had it not been for the detachment under Hanno, which now came suddenly into action. While the Gauls were in the height of their excitement in attempting to drive back the Carthaginians from the bank, they were thunderstruck at hearing the shouts and cries of an enemy behind them, and on looking around, they saw the troops of Hanno pouring down on them from the thickets with terrible recklessness and force. It is very difficult for an army to fight both in front and in the rear at the same time. The Gauls, after a brief struggle, abandoned the attempt any longer to oppose Hannibal's landing. They fled down the river and back into the interior, leaving Hanno in secure possession of the bank, while Hannibal and his forces came up at their leisure out of the water, finding friends instead of enemies to receive them.

The remainder of the army was to be transported next, and this was accomplished with little difficulty now that there was no enemy to disturb their operations. One part of the force, however, experienced some trouble and delay. It was a body of elephants which formed a part of the army. The question of how to get the unwieldy animals across so broad and rapid a river was difficult one. There are various accounts of how Hannibal accomplished the task. One method was as follows: the keeper of the elephants selected one more spirited and passionate in disposition than the rest and decided to tease and torment him so as to make him angry. The elephant advanced toward his keeper with his trunk raised to take vengeance. The keeper fled; the elephant pursued him, the other elephants of the herd following, as is the habit of the animal on such occasions. The keeper ran into the water as if to elude his pursuer, while the elephant and a large part of the herd pressed on after him. The man swam into the channel, and the elephants, before they could check themselves, found that they were beyond their depth. Some swam on after the keeper and crossed the river, where they were easily secured. Others, terrified, abandoned themselves to the current and were floated down, struggling helplessly as they went, until at last they grounded upon shallows or points of land, whence they gained the shore again, some on one side of the stream and some on the other.

This plan was only partially successful, and Hannibal devised a more effective method for the remainder of the troop. He built an immensely large raft, floated it up to the shore, fastened it there securely, and covered it with earth, turf, and bushes, so as to make it resemble a piece of the land. He then had a second raft constructed of the same size, which he brought up to the outer edge of the other, fastened it there by a temporary connection, and covered and concealed it as he had done the first. The first of these rafts extended two hundred feet from the shore and was fifty feet broad. The other, that is, the outer one, was only a little smaller. The soldiers then attempted to attract and drive the elephants over these rafts to the outer one, the animals imagining that they had not left the land. The two rafts were then disconnected from each other, and the outer one began to move with its bulky passengers over the water, towed by a number of boats which had previously been attached to its outer edge.

As soon as the elephants noticed the motion, they were alarmed and began immediately looking anxiously this way and that and crowding toward the edges of the raft which was carrying them away. They found themselves hemmed in by water on every side and were terrified and thrown into confusion. Some were crowded off the raft into the river, and drifted down until they landed below. The rest soon became calm and allowed themselves to be quietly ferried across the stream, when they found that all hope of escape and resistance were equally vain.

In the meantime, the troop of three hundred, which Scipio had sent up the river to see what news he could learn of the Carthaginians, were slowly making their way toward the point where Hannibal was crossing; and it happened that Hannibal had sent down a troop of five hundred, when he first reached the river, to see if they could learn any news of the Romans. Neither of the armies had any idea how near they were to the other. The two detachments met suddenly and unexpectedly on the way. They were sent to explore and not to fight; but as they were nearly equally matched, and each was ambitious of the glory of capturing the others and taking them as prisoners to their camp, they fought a long and bloody battle. A great number were killed, about the same amount on either side. The Romans

say they conquered. We do not know what the Carthaginians said, but as both parties retreated from the field and
went back to their respective camps, it is safe to assume
that neither could boast of a very decisive victory.

CHAPTER V

HANNIBAL CROSSES
THE ALPS.

T is difficult for anyone who has not actually seen such mountain scenery as is presented by the Alps to form any clear idea of its magnificence and grandeur. Hannibal had never seen the Alps, but the world was filled then, as now, with their fame.

Some of the leading features of perfection and grandeur which the mountains exhibit result mainly from the perpetual cold which rests on their summits. This is due simply to their elevation. In every part of the earth, as we ascend from the surface of the ground into the atmosphere, it becomes more and more cold, so that wherever we are, there rests an intense and perpetual cold, at a distance of only two or three miles above us. This is true not only in cool and temperate places on earth but also in the most oppressively hot regions. If we were to ascend in a balloon at Borneo at midday, when the burning sun of the tropics was directly over our heads, to an elevation of five or six miles,

we should find that although we had been moving nearer
to the sun all the time, its rays would have gradually lost
all their power. They would fall upon us as brightly as ever,
but their heat would be gone. They would feel like moon-
beams, and we should be surrounded with an atmosphere
as frosty as that of the icebergs of the Frigid Zone.

It is from this region of perpetual cold that hailstones
descend on us in the midst of summer, and snow is continually forming and falling there; but the light and fleecy flakes
melt before they reach the earth, so that, while the hail has
such solidity and momentum that it forces its way through,
the snow dissolves and falls on us as a cool and refreshing
rain. Rain cools the air around us and the ground because
it comes from cooler regions of the air above.

Now it happens that not only the summits but ex-
tensive portions of the upper slopes of the Alps rise into
the region of perpetual winter. Of course, water freezes
continually there, and the snow which forms falls to the
ground as snow and accumulates in vast and permanent
quantities. The summit of Mount Blanc is covered with
a bed of snow of enormous thickness, which is almost as
much a permanent geological layer of the mountain as the
granite which lies beneath it.

Of course, during the winter months, the whole country
of the Alps, valley as well as hill, is covered with snow. In
the spring the snow melts in the valleys and plains, and
higher up it becomes damp and heavy with partial melting and slides down the slopes in vast avalanches, which
sometimes are of such enormous magnitude and descend
with such resistless force as to bring down earth, rocks,
and even the trees of the forest in their path. On the higher
slopes, however, and over all the rounded summits, the
snow still clings to its place, yielding but very little to the
feeble beams of the sun, even in July.

There are vast ravines and valleys among the higher Alps where the snow accumulates, being driven into them by winds and storms in the winter and sliding into them, in great avalanches, in the spring. These vast deposits of snow are changed into ice below the surface; for at the surface there is a continual melting, and the water, flowing down through the mass, freezes below. Therefore there are valleys, or rather ravines, some of them two or three miles wide and ten or fifteen miles long, filled with ice, transparent, solid, and blue, hundreds of feet in depth. They are called glaciers. And what is most astonishing in respect to these icy heaps is that, though the ice is perfectly compact and solid, the whole mass is found to be continually in a state of slow motion down the valley in which it lies, at the rate of about a foot in twenty-four hours. By standing on the surface and listening attentively, we might hear, from time to time, a grinding sound. The rocks which lie along the sides are pulverized and are continually moving against each other and falling; a more direct and positive proof still of the motion of the mass is that a mark may be made on the ice, and marks corresponding to it made on the solid rocks on each side of the valley, and by this means the motion and the exact rate of movement may be calculated.

Therefore the valleys are really and literally rivers of ice, rising among the summits of the mountains and flowing, slowly but with a continuous and certain current, to a sort of mouth in some great and open valley below. Here the streams, which have flowed over the surface above and descended into the mass through countless crevices and chasms into which the traveler looks down with terror, converge and come out from under the ice in a muddy torrent, which comes out from a vast archway made by the falling in of masses which the water has undermined. This lower end of the glacier sometimes makes a vertical wall

hundreds of feet in height; sometimes it crowds down into
the fertile valley, advancing in some unusually cold summer into the cultivated country, where, as it slowly moves
on, it plows up the ground, carries away the orchards and
fields, and even drives the inhabitants from the villages
which it threatens. If the next summer proves warm, the
terrible monster slowly draws back its frigid head, and the
inhabitants return to the ground it reluctantly evacuates
and attempt to repair the damage it has done.

The Alps lie between France and Italy, and the great
valleys and the ranges of mountain land lie in such a direction that they must be crossed in order to pass from one
country to the other. These ranges are, however, not regular. They are divided by innumerable chasms, fissures,
and ravines; in some places they rise in vast rounded summits and swells, covered with fields of spotless snow; in
others they tower in lofty, needle-like peaks, which even
the chamois, a goatlike antelope, cannot scale, and where
scarcely a flake of snow can find a place of rest. Around
and among these peaks and summits and through these
frightful narrow passes and chasms, the roads twist and
turn, in a zigzagging and constantly ascending path, creeping along the most frightful steep mass of rock, sometimes
beneath them and sometimes on the brink. The roads pen-
etrate the darkest and gloomiest narrow passes, narrowly
miss the most impetuous and foaming torrents, and at last,
perhaps, emerge on the surface of a glacier, to be lost in
limitless fields of ice and snow, where countless brooks
run in glassy channels and crevasses yawn, ready to take
advantage of any slip which may enable them to take the
traveler down into their bottomless abysses.

And yet, notwithstanding the awful desolation which
dominates the upper regions of the Alps, the lower valleys,

through which the streams finally meander out into the open plains and by which the traveler gains access to the most perfect scenes of the upper mountains, are unbelievably green and beautiful. They are fertilized by the continual rain in the early spring, and the sun beats down into them with a pleasant warmth in summer, which brings out millions of flowers of the most beautiful forms and colors and ripens rapidly the broadest and richest fields of grain. Cottages of every picturesque and beautiful form, tenanted by the cultivators, the shepherds and the herdsmen, crown every little swell in the bottom of the valley and cling to the slopes of the mountains which rise on either hand. Above them, eternal forests of firs and pines wave, feathering over the steepest and most rocky slopes with their shadowy foliage. Still higher, gray masses of rock rise to form spires and pinnacles far grander and more picturesque, if not so symmetrically formed, than those constructed by man. Between those, in the background, are vast towering masses of white and dazzling snow, which crown the summits of the loftier mountains beyond.

Hannibal's determination to carry an army into Italy by way of the Alps, instead of transporting them by galleys over the sea, has always been regarded as one of the greatest undertakings of ancient times. He hesitated for some time about whether he should go down the Rhone and meet and give battle to Scipio, or whether he should leave the Roman army to its course and proceed directly toward the Alps and Italy. The officers and soldiers of the army, who had now learned something of their destination and of their leader's plans, wanted to go and meet the Romans. They dreaded the Alps. They were willing to encounter a military foe, however formidable, for this was a danger they were accustomed to and could understand;

but they imagined the terror of falling down the cliffs of ragged rocks or of gradually freezing and being buried half alive in eternal snows.

Hannibal, when he found that his soldiers were afraid to proceed, called the leading portions of his army together and spoke to them. He disapproved of them for yielding now to unworthy fears, after having successfully met and triumphed over such dangers as they had already incurred. "You have ascended the Pyrenees," said he. "You have crossed the Rhone. You are now actually in sight of the Alps, which are the very gates of access to the country of the enemy. What do you believe the Alps to be? They are nothing but high mountains, after all. Suppose they are higher than the Pyrenees, they do not reach to the skies; and since they do not, they cannot be insurmountable. They are surmounted, in fact, every day; they are even inhabited and cultivated, and travelers continually pass over them. And what a single man can do, an army can do, for an army is only a large number of single men. In fact, to a soldier, who has nothing to carry with him but the implements of war, no way can be too difficult to be surmounted by courage and energy."

After finishing his speech, Hannibal, finding his men restored to confidence and encouraged by what he had said, ordered them to go to their tents and refresh themselves and prepare to march the following day. They made no further opposition to going on. Hannibal did not, however, proceed at once directly toward the Alps. He did not know what the plans of Scipio might be, who, it will be recollected, was below him on the Rhone with the Roman army. He did not wish to waste his time and his strength in a contest with Scipio in Gaul but to press on and get across the Alps into Italy as soon as possible. And so, fearing that

Scipio could strike across the country and intercept him
if he should attempt to go by the most direct route, he
decided to move northward up the River Rhone, until he
was well into the interior, with a view of reaching the Alps
ultimately by a more indirect journey.

It was Scipio's plan to reach Hannibal and attack him
as soon as possible; and as soon as his horsemen, or rather,
those who were left alive after the battle, had returned and
informed him that Hannibal and his army were near, he
put his camp in motion and moved rapidly up the river. He
arrived at the place where the Carthaginians had crossed
a few days after they had gone. The spot was in a terrible
state of ruin and confusion. The grass and vegetation were
trampled down in a circle a mile wide, and all over the
space were spots of black and smoldering remains, where
the campfires had been burning. The tops and branches
of trees lay everywhere around, their leaves withering in
the sun, and the groves and forests were burdened with
limbs and rejected trunks and fallen trees left where they
lay. The shore was lined far down the stream with ruins
of boats and rafts, with weapons which had been lost or
abandoned, and with the bodies of those who had been
drowned in the passage or killed in the battle on the shore.
These and numerous other signs remained but the army
was gone.

There were groups of natives and other visitors who
had come to look at the spot now destined to become so
memorable in history. From these men Scipio learned when
and where Hannibal had gone. He decided that it was useless to attempt to pursue him. He was greatly perplexed to
know what to do. In the casting of lots, Spain had fallen
to him, but now that the great enemy whom he had come
forward to meet had left Spain altogether, his only hope

of intercepting his progress was to sail back into Italy and meet him as he came down from the Alps into the great valley of the Po. Still, as Spain had been assigned to him as his province, he could not entirely abandon it. He sent forward the largest part of his army into Spain to attack the forces that Hannibal had left there, while he himself, with a smaller force, went down to the seashore and sailed back to Italy again. He expected to find Roman forces in the valley of the Po, with which he hoped to be strong enough to meet Hannibal as he descended from the mountains, if he should succeed in making a passage over them.

In the meantime, Hannibal went on, drawing nearer and nearer to the ranges of snowy summits which his soldiers had seen for many days in their eastern horizon. These ranges were shining brilliantly when the sun went down in the west, for then it shined directly on them. As the army approached nearer to the ranges, the mountain peaks gradually withdrew from sight and disappeared, being concealed by less lofty summits. As the soldiers went on and began to pass into the valleys and draw near to the awful chasms and precipices among the mountains and saw the muddy torrents descending from them, their fears revived. It was, however, now too late to retreat. They pressed forward; ascending continually, until their road grew extremely steep and insecure, threading its way through almost impassable narrow passages with rugged cliffs overhanging them and snowy summits towering all around.

At last they came to a narrow spot in the mountains through which it was necessary to pass, but which was guarded by large bodies of armed men assembled on the rocks and cliffs above ready to hurl stones and weapons of every kind upon them if they should attempt to pass through. The army halted. Hannibal ordered them to camp where they were, until he could consider what to do. In the course of the day he learned that the mountaineers did not remain at their elevated posts during the night, on account of the intense cold and exposure. He also knew that it would be impossible for an army to make it through such a pass without daylight to guide them. The road, or rather pathway, which passes through these narrow spots, follows generally the course of a mountain torrent, which flows through a succession of frightful ravines and chasms, and often passes along on a shelf or cliff of the rock, hundreds and sometimes thousands of feet from the bed of the stream, which foams and roars far below. There could, of course, be no hope of passing safely by such a route without the light of day.

The mountaineers, therefore, knowing that it was not necessary to guard the pass at night—its own terrible danger being then a sufficient protection—were accustomed to disperse in the evening and descend to regions where they could find shelter and rest and to return and renew their watch in the morning. When Hannibal learned this, he decided to act quickly in getting up the rocks the next day before them, and in order to prevent them from figuring out his plan, he pretended to be making all the arrangements for camping for the night on the ground he had taken. He pitched more tents and built, toward evening, a great many fires, and he began some preparations which indicated that it was his intention to force his way through the pass the next day. He moved forward a strong detachment up to a point near the entrance to the pass and put them in a fortified position there, as if to have them all ready to advance when the proper time should arrive on the following day.

The mountaineers, seeing all these preparations going on, looked forward to a conflict the next day and, during the night, left their positions as usual to descend to places of shelter. The next morning, however, when they began at an early hour to ascend to their position again, they were astonished to find all the lofty rocks and cliffs which over-hung the pass covered with Carthaginians. Hannibal had awakened a strong body of his men at the earliest dawn and led them up the steep climb to the places which the mountaineers had left, so as to be there before them. The mountaineers paused, astonished at this sight, and their disappointment and rage increased on looking down into the valley below and seeing there the remainder of the Carthaginian army quietly moving through the pass in a long column, safe apparently from any interference, since friends, and not enemies, were now in possession of the cliffs above.

The mountaineers could not restrain their feelings of frustration and anger but immediately rushed down the slopes which they had in part ascended and attacked the army in the pass. An awful scene of struggle and confu-sion followed. Some were killed by weapons or by rocks rolled down upon them. Others, contending together and struggling desperately in places of very narrow foothold, tumbled headlong down the rugged rocks into the tor-rent below; and horses, laden with baggage and stores, became frightened and unmanageable and crowded each other over the most frightful cliffs. Hannibal, who was above on the higher rocks, looked down upon this scene for a time with great anxiety and terror. He did not dare to descend and mingle in the battle, for fear of increasing the confusion. He soon found, however, that it was abso-lutely necessary for him to intervene, and he came down as rapidly as possible, leading his detachment with him. They descended by winding and zigzag paths, wherever they could get footing among the rocks, and attacked the mountaineers with great fury. The result was, as he had feared, much confusion and slaughter. The horses were more and more terrified by the fresh energy of the combat and by the sound of louder shouts and cries, which were made doubly terrific by the echoes of the mountains. They crowded against each other and fell, horses and men together, in masses over the cliffs to the rugged rocks below, where they lay in confusion, some dead, and others dying, writhing helplessly in agony or vainly endeavoring to crawl away.

The mountaineers were, however, conquered and driven away at last, and the pass was left clear. The Carthaginian column was restored to order. The horses that had not fallen were calmed and quieted. The baggage which had been thrown down was gathered up, and the wounded men were placed on stretchers, rudely constructed on the spot, that they might be carried to a place of safety. In a short time all were ready to move on, and the march began again. There was no further difficulty. The column advanced in a quiet and orderly manner until they had made it through the pass. At the farthest point of it they came to a spacious fort belonging to the natives. Hannibal took possession of the fort and paused for a little time there to rest and refresh his men.

One of the greatest difficulties encountered by a general in conducting an army through difficult and dangerous roads is that of providing food for them. An army can transport its own food only a short way. Men traveling over smooth roads can only carry provisions for a few days, and where the roads are as difficult and dangerous as the passes of the Alps, they can scarcely carry any. Therefore, a commander must find provisions in the country through which he is marching. Hannibal had not only to look out for the safety of his men, but their food was exhausted, and he had to take immediate measures to secure a supply.

The lower slopes of lofty mountains usually afford abundant food for flocks and herds. The showers which are continually falling there, and the moisture which comes down the sides of the mountains through the ground, keep the turf perpetually green. Sheep and cattle love to pasture on it; they climb to great heights, finding the vegetation finer and sweeter the higher they go. Thus the inhabitants of mountain ranges are almost always shepherds and herdsmen. Grain can be raised in the valleys below, but the slopes of the mountains, though they produce grass to perfection, are too steep to be tilled.

As soon as Hannibal was established in the fort, he sent around small bodies of men to seize and drive in all the cattle and sheep they could find. These men were, of course, armed, in order that they might be prepared to meet any resistance they might encounter. The mountaineers, however, did not attempt to resist them. They felt that they had been conquered, and as a result they were disheartened and discouraged. The only method of saving the cattle which was left to them was to drive them as fast as they could into concealed and inaccessible places. They attempted to do this, and while Hannibal's parties were searching the valleys all around them, examining every field and barn, and sheepfold they could find, the unfortunate and despairing inhabitants were flying in all directions, driving the cows and sheep, on which their whole hope of a livelihood depended, into the security of the mountains. They urged them into wild thickets, dark ravines and chasms, over dangerous glaciers and up the steepest ascents, wherever there was the readiest prospect of getting them out of the plunderer's way.

The attempts to save what little property they had were not very successful. Hannibal's marauding parties kept coming back to camp, one after another, with droves of sheep and cattle before them, some larger and some smaller, but making up a vast amount in all. Hannibal fed his men three days on the food thus obtained for them. It requires an enormous amount to feed ninety or a hundred thousand men, even for three days; besides, in all such cases as this, an army wastes and destroys far more than they really consume.

During the three days the army was not fixed in one place but was moving slowly on. The way, though still difficult and dangerous, was at least open before them, as there was now no enemy to oppose their passage. So they went on, wasting the abundant supplies they had obtained and rejoicing in the double victory they were gaining, over the hostility of the people and the physical dangers and difficulties of the way. The poor mountaineers returned to their cabins ruined and desolate, for mountaineers who have lost their cows and their sheep have lost everything.

The Alps are not all in Switzerland. Some of the most celebrated peaks and ranges are in France and Italy. But in the time of the Romans, the whole area was divided into small states called *cantons*. In his march onward from the pass, Hannibal soon approached the boundaries of another canton. As he was advancing slowly into it, with the long column of his army winding up with him through the valleys, he was met at the borders of this new state by a delegation sent from their government. They brought with them fresh stores of provisions and a number of guides. They said that they had heard of the terrible destruction which had come on the other canton in consequence of their effort to oppose his progress and that they had no intention of renewing so vain an attempt. They came, therefore, to offer Hannibal their friendship and their aid. They had brought guides to show the army the best way over the mountains and a present of provisions; and to prove the sincerity of their declaration they offered Hannibal hostages. These hostages were young men and boys, the sons of the principal inhabitants, whom they offered to deliver into Hannibal's power to be kept by him until he should see that they were faithful and true in doing what they offered.

Hannibal was so accustomed to clever schemes and treachery that he was at first very much at a loss to decide whether these offers and declarations were honest and sincere or whether they were only made to put him off his guard. He thought it possible that their plan was to lead him into some dangerous pass or labyrinth of rocks from which he could not escape, where they could attack and destroy him. He decided to return them a favorable answer but to watch them very carefully and to proceed under their guidance with the utmost caution and care. He accepted the provisions they offered and took the hostages. These last he delivered into the custody of a body of his soldiers, and they marched on with the rest of the army. Then, directing the new guides to lead the way, the army moved on after them. The elephants went first, with a moderate force for their protection preceding and accompanying them. Then came long columns of horses and mules, loaded with military stores and baggage, and finally the foot soldiers followed, marching irregularly in a long column. The whole column must have extended many miles and must have appeared from any of the hills around like an enormous serpent, winding its way along the twists and turns of the path through the wild and desolate valleys.

Hannibal was right in his suspicions. The delegation was a clever scheme. The men who sent it had laid in ambush in a very narrow pass, concealing their troops in thickets and in chasms, in nooks and corners among the rugged rocks, and when the guides had led the army well into the danger, a sudden signal was given, and concealed enemies rushed down upon them in great numbers, breaking into their ranks, and repeating the scene of terrible uproar, tumult, and destruction which had been witnessed in the other pass. One would have thought that the elephants, being so unwieldy and so helpless in such a scene, would have been the first objects of attack. But it was not so. The mountaineers were afraid of them. They had never seen such animals before, and they felt for them a mysterious awe, not knowing what terrible powers such enormous beasts might be expected to wield. They kept away from them, therefore, and from the horsemen and poured down upon the column of foot soldiers which followed in the rear.

They were quite successful at the beginning. They broke through the head of the column and drove the rest back. The horses and elephants, in the meantime, moved forward, bearing the baggage with them, so that the two portions of the army were soon entirely separated. Hannibal was behind with the soldiers. The mountaineers made good their position, and as night came on, the battle ceased, for in such wilds as these no one can move at all, except with the light of day. The mountaineers, however, remained in their place, dividing the army, and Hannibal waited, during the night, in a state of great suspense and anxiety with the elephants and the baggage separated from him, and apparently at the mercy of the enemy.

During the night he made vigorous preparations for attacking the mountaineers the next day. As soon as the morning light appeared, he made the attack, and he succeeded in driving the enemy away, so far, at least, as to allow him to get his army together again. He then began once more to move on. The mountaineers, however, hovered over him along the way and did all they could to intervene and complicate his march. They concealed themselves for ambush and attacked the Carthaginians as they passed. They rolled stones down on them or discharged spears and arrows from cliffs above; and if any of Hannibal's army became, for any reason, detached from the rest, they would cut off their retreat and then take them prisoners or destroy them. Thus they gave Hannibal a great deal of trouble. They complicated his march continually, without presenting at any point a force which he could meet and encounter in battle. Of course, Hannibal could no longer trust his guides, and he was obliged to make his way as he best could, sometimes right, but often wrong, and exposed to a thousand difficulties and dangers, which those acquainted with the country might have easily avoided. All this time the mountaineers were continually attacking him, in bands like those of robbers, sometimes in the forefront of his division and sometimes in the rear, wherever the nature of the ground or the circumstances of the marching army afforded them an opportunity.

Hannibal continued steadfastly, however, through all these discouragements, protecting his men as far as it was in his power but pressing earnestly on, until in nine days he reached the summit. Not the summit of the mountains, but the summit of the *pass*—the highest point which it was necessary for him to attain in going over. In all mountain ranges there are depressions, which in Switzerland are called *necks,* and the pathways and roads over the ranges always lie in these. In America, such a depression in a ridge of land, if well-marked, is called a *notch.* Hannibal attained the highest point of the mountain range by which he was to pass over, in nine days after the great battle. There were, of course, lofty peaks and summits towering still far above him.

He camped there two days to rest and refresh his men. The enemy no longer intervened. In fact, parties were continually coming into the camp, men and horses that had been lost or left in the valleys below. They came in slowly, some wounded, others exhausted by fatigue and exposure. In some cases horses came in alone. They were horses that had slipped or stumbled and fallen among the rocks, or had sunk down exhausted by their toil and had been left behind. After recovering their strength, they had followed on, led by a strange instinct to keep to the tracks which their companions had made, and they rejoined the camp at last in safety.

In fact, one great reason for Hannibal's delay at his camp on or near the summit of the pass was to afford time for all the missing men to join the army again, those that had the power to do so. Had it not been for this necessity, he would doubtless have descended some distance, at least, to a warmer more sheltered position before seeking rest. A more gloomy and desolate resting place than the summit of an Alpine pass can scarcely be found. The barren rocks are entirely destitute of vegetation, and they had lost the picturesque forms which they assume further below. They spread in vast, naked fields in every direction, rising in gentle slopes, bleak and dreary, the surface whitened as if bleached by the constant rains. Storms are almost perpetual in those elevated regions. The vast cloud which, to the eye of the shepherd in the valley below, seems only a fleecy cap resting serenely upon the summit or slowly floating along the sides, is really a driving mist or cold and stormy rain, howling dismally over unending fields of broken rocks, as if angry that it can make nothing grow on them, with all its watering. Therefore there are seldom distant views to be obtained, and everything near presents a scene of simple dreariness and desolation.

Hannibal's soldiers found themselves in the midst of a dismal scene in their lofty camp. There is one special source of danger, too, in such places as this, which the lower portions of the mountains are less exposed to, and that is the entire obliteration of the pathway by falls of snow. It seems almost absurd to speak of pathways in such regions, where there is no turf to be worn, and the boundless fields of rocks, ragged and hard, will take no trace of footsteps. There are, however, generally some faint traces of the path, and where these fail entirely the path is sometimes marked by small piles of stones, placed at intervals along the line of route. An unpracticed eye would scarcely distinguish these little landmarks from accidental heaps of stones which lie everywhere around. However, they render a very essential service to the guides and to the mountaineers, who have been accustomed to taking their steps by similar assistance in other portions of the mountains.

But when snow begins to fall, all these and every other possible means of distinguishing the way are soon entirely obliterated. The whole surface of the ground, or rather of the rocks, is covered, and all landmarks disappear. The little monuments become nothing but slight differences in the surface of the snow, not unlike a thousand others. The air is thick and murky and shuts off all distant views and the shape and form of the land that is near; the bewildered traveler does not even have the stars to guide him, as there is nothing to be seen in the sky but dark, falling flakes, descending from a thick canopy of stormy clouds.

Hannibal encountered a snowstorm while on the summit of the pass, and his army was terrified by it. It was now November. The army had met with so many delays that their journey could not be postponed. It would be unsafe to wait until the snow should melt again. As soon as the storm ended and the clouds cleared away, so as to allow the men to see the general features of the country around, the camp was broken up and the army put in motion. The soldiers marched through the snow with great anxiety and fear. Men went on ahead to explore the way and to guide the rest by flags and banners which they bore. Those who went first made paths for those who followed behind, as the snow was trampled down by their footsteps. Regardless of these aids, however, the army moved on with extreme care and much fear.

Finally, after descending a short distance, Hannibal thought they must soon come in sight of the Italian valleys and plains which lay beyond the Alps. He went forward among the pioneers, who had charge of the banners by which the movements of the army were directed, and as soon as the open country began to come into view, he selected a spot where the widest view was presented and halted his army there to let them take a view of the beautiful country which now lay before them. The Alps are very steep on the Italian side. The descent is very sudden, from the cold and icy summits to a broad expanse of the most abundant and sunny plains. Upon these plains, which were spread out in a most enchanting landscape at their feet, Hannibal and his soldiers now looked down with exultation and delight. Beautiful lakes, studded with still more beautiful islands, reflected the beams of the sun. An end-less succession of fields in sober autumn colors, with the cottages of the laborers and stacks of grain scattered here and there upon them, and rivers meandering through ver-dant meadows gave variety and enchantment to the view.

Hannibal made an address to his officers and men, con-gratulating them on having arrived, at last, so near to a suc-cessful ending of their toils. "The difficulties of the way," he said, "are at last surmounted, and these mighty barriers that we have scaled are the walls, not only of Italy, but of Rome itself. Since we have passed the Alps, the Romans will have no remaining protection against us. It is only one battle, when we get down on the plains, or at most two, and the great city itself will be entirely at our disposal."

The whole army was excited and encouraged, both by the beauty which presented itself to their view and by the words of Hannibal. They prepared for the descent, antici-pating little difficulty; but they found, on restarting their march, that their troubles were by no means over. The mountains are far steeper on the Italian side than on the other, and it was extremely difficult to find paths by which the elephants and the horses, and even the men, could safely descend. They moved on for some time with great labor and fatigue, until Hannibal, looking on before, found that the head of the column had stopped, and the whole train behind was soon jammed together, the ranks halting along the way in succession, as they found their path blocked up by the halting of those before them.

Hannibal sent forward to determine the cause of the difficulty and found that the front division of the army had reached a cliff that was impossible to descend. It was necessary to return the way they had come in hopes of find-ing some practical way of getting down. The guides and pioneers went on, leading the army after them, and soon

got upon a glacier which lay in their way. There was fresh
snow upon the surface, covering the ice and concealing
the crevasses, as they are termed—that is, the great cracks
and fissures which extend in the glaciers down through
the body of the ice. The army moved on, trampling down
the new snow and making at first a good roadway by their
footsteps; but very soon the old ice and snow became trampled up by the hoofs of the horses and the heavy tread of
such vast multitudes of armed men. It softened to a great
depth and made moving through it an enormous labor.
Besides, the surface of the ice and snow sloped steeply,
and the men and beasts were continually falling or sliding down and getting swallowed up in avalanches which
their own weight set in motion or falling into concealed
crevasses where they sank to rise no more.

They, however, made some progress, though slowly
and with great danger. They at last got below the region of
the snow, but here they encountered new difficulties in the
abruptness and ruggedness of the rocks and in the zigzag
and tortuous direction of the way. At last they came to a
spot where their further progress appeared to be entirely
cut off by a large mass of rock, which it seemed necessary to remove in order to widen the passage sufficiently
to allow them to go on. The Roman historians say that
Hannibal removed these rocks by building great fires on
them, and then pouring on vinegar, which opened seams
and fissures in them, which allowed the rocks to be split
and pried to pieces with wedges and crowbars. On read-
ing this account, the mind naturally pauses to consider
the likelihood of it being true. As they had no gunpowder
in those days, they were compelled to resort to some such
method as the one above described for removing rocks.
Some species of rock are easily cracked and broken by the

action of fire. Others resist it. There seems, however, to be no obvious reason why vinegar should materially assist in the operation. Besides, we cannot suppose that Hannibal could have had, at such a time and place, large supplies of vinegar on hand. On the whole, it is possible that, if any such operation was performed at all, it was on a very small scale, and the results must have been very insignificant at the time, though the fact has since been greatly celebrated in history.

In coming over the snow and in descending the rocks immediately below, the army, and especially the animals, suffered a great deal from hunger. It was difficult to find food of any kind for them. They continued their descent and finally came first into the region of forests and soon after to slopes of grassy fields descending into warm and fertile valleys. Here the animals were allowed to stop and rest and renew their strength by an abundance of food. The men rejoiced that their toils and dangers were over, and descending easily the remainder of the way, they camped at last safely on the plains of Italy.

CHAPTER VI

HANNIBAL IN THE NORTH OF ITALY.

HEN Hannibal's army found themselves on the plains of Italy and sat down quietly to rest, they felt the effects of their fatigues and exposures far more than while actually on the mountains. They were, in fact, in a miserable condition. Hannibal told a Roman officer whom he afterward took prisoner that more than thirty thousand perished on the way in crossing the mountains; some were lost in the battles which were fought in the passes and a greater number still, probably, from exposure to fatigue and cold and from falls among the rocks and glaciers and diseases produced by destitution and misery. The remnant of the army which was left on reaching the plain were starving, sickly, ragged, and spiritless, far more inclined to lie down and die than to go on and undertake the conquest of Italy and Rome.

After some days, however, they began to strengthen. Although they had been half-starved on the mountains, they now had plenty of wholesome food. They repaired their tattered garments and their broken weapons. They talked with one another about the terrific experiences through which they'd passed, and the dangers which they'd surmounted, and in this way, gradually strengthening their impressions of the greatness of the exploits they had performed, they began soon to awaken in each other an ambition to go on and undertake the accomplishment of other deeds of daring and glory.

We left Scipio with his army at the mouth of the Rhone about to set sail for Italy with a part of his force, while the rest of it was sent on toward Spain. Scipio sailed along the coast by Genoa and then to Pisa where he landed. He stopped a little while to strengthen his soldiers after the voyage and in the meantime sent orders to all the Roman forces then in the north of Italy to join his unit. He hoped in this way to collect a force strong enough to encounter Hannibal. These arrangements being made, he marched to the north as rapidly as possible. He knew in what condition Hannibal's army had descended from the Alps and hoped to attack them before they had time to recover from the effects of their lack of basic necessities and sufferings. He reached the Po before he saw anything of Hannibal.

Hannibal, in the meantime, was not idle. As soon as his men were in a condition to move, he began to act on the tribes that he found at the foot of the mountains, offering his friendship to some and attacking others. He conquered those who attempted to resist him, moving, all the time, gradually southward toward the Po. That river has numerous branches, and among them is one named the Ticinus. It was on the banks of this river that the two armies at last came together.

Both generals must have felt some degree of anxiety in respect to the result of the battle which was about to take place. Scipio knew very well Hannibal's terrible efficiency as a warrior, and he was himself a general of great distinction, and a Roman, so that Hannibal had no reason to anticipate a very easy victory. But whatever doubts or fears generals may feel on the eve of a battle, it is always considered necessary to conceal them entirely from the men and to motivate and encourage the troops with a most undoubting confidence that they will gain the victory.

Both Hannibal and Scipio made speeches to their respective armies—at least so say the historians of those times—each one expressing to his followers the certainty that the other side would easily be beaten. The speech attributed to Scipio was somewhat as follows:

"I wish to say a few words to you, soldiers, before we go into battle. It is, perhaps, scarcely necessary. It certainly would not be necessary if I had now under my command the same troops that I took with me to the mouth of the Rhone. They knew the Carthaginians there and would not have feared them here. A body of our horsemen met and attacked a larger body of theirs and defeated them. We then advanced with our whole force toward their encampment, in order to give them battle. They, however, abandoned the ground and retreated before we reached the spot, acknowledging, by their flight, their own fear and our superiority. If you were with us there and witnessed these facts, there would have be no need that I should say anything to convince you now how easily you are going to defeat this Carthaginian foe.

"We have had a war with this same nation before. We conquered them then, both by land and sea; and when finally peace was made, we required them to pay us tribute, and we continued to exact it from them for twenty years. They are a conquered nation; and now this miserable army has forced its way insanely over the Alps, just to throw itself into our hands. They meet us reduced in numbers and exhausted in resources and strength. More than half of their army perished in the mountains, and those that survived are weak, dispirited, ragged, and diseased. And yet they are compelled to meet us. If there was any chance for retreat or any possible way for them to avoid the necessity of a battle, they would availed themselves of it. But there is not. They are hemmed in by the mountains, which are now, to them, an impassable wall, for they have not strength to scale them again. They are not real enemies; they are the mere remnants and shadows of enemies. They are totally disheartened and discouraged, their strength and energy, both of soul and body, being spent and gone, through the cold, the hunger, and the squalid misery they have endured. Their joints are numb, their sinews stiffened, and their forms emaciated. Their armor is shattered and broken, their horses are lamed, and all their equipment is worn out and ruined, so that really what I fear most is that the world will refuse us the glory of the victory and say that it was the Alps that conquered Hannibal, and not the Roman army.

"Easy as the victory is to be, however, we must remember that there is a great deal at stake in the contest. It is not merely for glory that we are now about to contend. If Hannibal conquers, he will march to Rome, and our wives, our children, and all that we hold dear will be at his mercy. Remember this, and go into the battle feeling that the fate of Rome itself is depending on the result."

A speech is attributed to Hannibal, too, on the occasion of this battle. He showed, however, his characteristic ingenuity and spirit of scheming in the way in which he managed to attract strong attention to what he was going to say, by the manner in which he introduced it. He formed his army into a circle, as if to witness a spectacle. He then brought into the center of this circle a number of prisoners that he had taken among the Alps—perhaps they were the hostages which had been delivered to him, as related in the previous chapter. Hannibal had brought them with his army down into Italy, and now, introducing them into the center of the circle which the army formed, he threw down before them such arms as they were accustomed to use in their native mountains and asked them whether they would be willing to take those weapons and fight each other, on condition that each one who killed his antagonist should be restored to his liberty and have a horse and armor given him, so that he could return home with honor. The prisoners said readily that they would and seized the arms with great eagerness. Two or three pairs of combatants were allowed to fight. One of each pair was killed, and the other set at liberty according to Hannibal's promise. The combatants excited the greatest interest and awakened the strongest enthusiasm among the soldiers who witnessed them. When this effect had been sufficiently produced, the rest of the prisoners were sent away, and Hannibal addressed the vast ring of soldiers as follows:

"I have intended, soldiers, in what you have now seen, not merely to amuse you but to give you a picture of your own situation. You are hemmed in on the right and left by two seas, and you have not so much as a single ship on either of them. Then there is the Po before you and the Alps behind. The Po is a deeper and more rapid and turbulent river than the Rhone; as for the Alps, it was with the utmost difficulty that you passed over them when you were in full strength and vigor; they are an insurmountable wall to you now. You are therefore shut in, like our prisoners, on every side, and have no hope of life and liberty but in battle and victory.

"The victory, however, will not be difficult. I see, wherever I look amongst you, a spirit of determination and courage which I am sure will make you conquerors. The troops which you are going to contend against are mostly fresh recruits that know nothing of the discipline of the camp and can never successfully confront such war-worn veterans as you. You all know each other well, and me. I was, in fact, a pupil with you for many years before I took the command. But Scipio's forces are strangers to one another and to him and, consequently, have no common bond of sympathy; as for Scipio himself, his very commission as a Roman general is only six months old.

"Think, too, what a splendid and prosperous career victory will open before you. It will conduct you to Rome. It will make you masters of one of the most powerful and wealthy cities in the world. Thus far you have fought your battles only for glory or for dominion; now, you will have something more substantial to reward your success. There will be great treasures to be divided among you if we conquer, but if we are defeated, we are lost. Hemmed in as we are on every side, there is no place that we can reach by flight. There is, therefore, no such alternative as flight left to us. *We must conquer.*"

It is hardly possible that Hannibal could have really and honestly felt all the confidence that he expressed in his speech to his soldiers. He must have had some fears. In fact, in all enterprises undertaken by man, the indications of success and the hopes based upon them, will rise and fall from time to time and cause his confidence as a result to ebb and flow, so that bright anticipations of success and triumph will alternate in his heart with feelings of discouragement and despondency. This effect is experienced by all—by the energetic and decided as well as the timid and the faltering. The former, however, never allow the rise and fall of hope and fear to influence their actions. They consider well the solid grounds for expecting success before beginning an undertaking and then go steadily forward, under all aspects of the sky—when it shines and when it rains—until they reach the end. The inefficient and undecided can act only under present hope. The end they aim at must be visible at all times. If for a moment it passes out of view, their motive is gone, and they can do no more, until, by some change in circumstances, it comes in sight again.

Hannibal was energetic and decided. The time for him to consider whether he would encounter the hostility of the Roman empire, stirred to the highest possible degree, was when his army was drawn up upon the banks of the Iberus, before they crossed it. The Iberus was his Rubicon. Once that line was crossed, there was to be no further faltering. The difficulties, which came up from time to time to throw a cloud over his prospects, only seemed to stimulate him to fresh energy and to awaken a new, though still a calm and steady, resolution. It was so at the Pyrenees; it was so at the Rhone; it was so among the Alps, where the difficulties and dangers would have induced almost any other commander to have returned; and it was still so now that he found himself shut in on every side by the stern boundaries of Northern Italy, which he could not possibly hope to pass again, and the whole disposable force of the Roman empire, commanded too by one of the consuls, concentrated before him. The imminent danger produced no faltering and apparently no fear.

The armies were not yet in sight of each other. They were, in fact, on opposite sides of the River Po. The Roman commander decided to march his troops across the river and advance in search of Hannibal, who was still at some distance. After considering the various means of crossing the stream, he finally decided to build a bridge.

Military commanders generally throw some sort of a bridge across a stream of water lying in their way if it is too deep to be easily crossed, unless it is so wide and rapid as to make the construction of the bridge difficult or impractical. In this latter case they cross as well as they can by means of boats and rafts and swimming. The Po, though not a very large stream at this point, was too deep to be crossed, and Scipio consequently built a bridge. The soldiers cut down the trees which grew in the forests along the banks, and after trimming off the tops and branches, they rolled the trunks into the water. They placed these trunks side by side, with others laid across them and pinned down on the top. In this way they formed rafts, which they placed in a line across the stream, securing them well to each other and to the banks. This made the foundation for the bridge, which they then covered with other materials, so as to make the upper surface a convenient roadway. The army was marched across it, and then a small detachment of soldiers was stationed at each end of it as a guard.

Such a bridge as this answers a very good temporary purpose, and in still water, as, for example, over narrow lakes or very sluggish streams, where there is very little current, a floating structure of this kind is sometimes built for permanent service. Such bridges will not, however, stand on broad and rapid rivers liable to floods. The pressure of the water alone, in such cases, would endanger all the fastenings; and in cases where driftwood or ice is brought down by the stream, the floating masses, not being able to pass under the bridge, would accumulate above it and would soon bear on it with such enormous pressure that nothing could withstand its force. The bridge would be broken away, and the whole—bridge, driftwood, and ice— would be carried irresistibly down the stream together.

Scipio's bridge, however, answered very well for his purpose. His army passed over it in safety. When Hannibal heard of this, he knew that the battle was at hand. Hannibal was himself at this time about five miles away. While Scipio was at work on the bridge, Hannibal was employed, mainly, as he had been all the time since his descent from the mountains, in conquering the various petty nations and tribes north of the Po. Some of them were willing to join his unit. Others were allies of the Romans and wished to remain so. He made treaties and sent help to the former and dispatched detachments of troops to intimidate and subdue the latter. When, however, he learned that Scipio had crossed the river, he ordered all these detachments to come immediately in, and he began to prepare in earnest for the impending battle.

He called together an assembly of his soldiers and announced to them finally that the battle was now near. He renewed the words of encouragement that he had spoken before, and in addition to what he then said, he now promised the soldiers rewards in land in case they proved victorious. "I will give you each a farm," said he, "wherever you choose to have it, either in Africa, Italy, or Spain. If, instead of the land, any of you shall prefer to receive an equivalent in money, you shall have the reward in that form, and then you can return home and live with your friends, as before the war, under circumstances which will make you objects of envy to those who remained behind. If any of you would like to live in Carthage, I will have you made free citizens, so that you can live there in independence and honor."

But what security would there be for the faithful fulfillment of these promises? In modern times such security is
given by bonds with financial penalties or by the deposit of
titles to property in responsible hands. In ancient days they
managed differently. The person making the promise bound
himself by some solemn and formal method of appeal, accompanied, in important cases, with certain ceremonies,
which were supposed to seal and confirm the obligation
assumed. In this case Hannibal brought a lamb in the presence of the assembled army. He held it before them with his
left hand, while with his right he grasped a heavy stone. He
then called aloud upon the gods, imploring them to destroy
him as he was about to slay the lamb, if he failed to perform
faithfully and fully the pledges that he had made. He then
struck the poor lamb a heavy blow with the stone. The
animal fell dead at his feet, and Hannibal was then bound,
in the opinion of the army, by a very solemn obligation
indeed, to be faithful in fulfilling his word.

The soldiers were filled with boldness and courage and
excited by these promises and were eager to have the battle
begin. The Roman soldiers, it seems, were in a different
state of mind. Some circumstances had occurred which
they considered bad omens, and they were dispirited and
depressed by them. It is astonishing that men should ever
allow their minds to be affected by such totally accidental
occurrences as these were. One of them was this: a wolf
came into their camp from one of the forests near and, after
wounding several men, made his escape again. The other
was more frivolous still. A swarm of bees flew into the camp
and landed on a tree just over Scipio's tent. This was considered, for some reason or other, a sign that some calamity
was going to happen to them, and the men were intimidated
and disheartened. They consequently looked forward to the

battle with uneasiness and anxiety, while the army of Hannibal anticipated it with eagerness and pleasure.

The battle came on very suddenly and at a moment when neither party was expecting it. A large detachment of both armies was advancing toward the position of the other, near the River Ticinus, to observe the enemies strength, when they met, and the battle began. Hannibal advanced with great sudden action and sent, at the same time, a detachment around to attack his enemy in the rear. The Romans soon began to fall into confusion: the horsemen and foot soldiers became tangled together; the men were trampled by the horses; and the horses were frightened by the men. In the midst of this scene, Scipio received a wound. A consul was a dignitary of very high consideration. He was, in fact, a sort of semi-king. The officers, and all the soldiers, as fast as they heard that the consul was wounded, were terrified and dismayed, and the Romans began to retreat. Scipio had a young son, also named Scipio, who was then about twenty years of age. He was fighting by the side of his father when he received his wound. He protected his father, got him into the center of a compact body of cavalry, and moved slowly off the ground, with those in the rear facing toward the enemy and beating them back, as they pressed on in pursuit of them. In this way they reached their camp. Here they stopped for the night. They had fortified the place, and as night was coming on, Hannibal thought it not wise to press on and attack them there. He waited for the morning. Scipio, however, himself wounded and his army discouraged, thought it not wise for him to wait until the morning. At midnight he put his whole force in motion to retreat. He kept the campfires burning and did everything else in his power to prevent the Carthaginians observing any signs of his departure. His army marched secretly and silently until they reached the river. They crossed it by the bridge they had built, and then, cutting away the fastenings by which the different rafts were held together, the structure was at once destroyed, and the pieces floated away, a mere mass of ruins, down the stream. From the Ticinus they floated, we may imagine, into the Po and then down the Po into the Adriatic Sea, where they drifted about until they were at last, one after another driven by storms on to the sandy shores.

CHAPTER VII

THE APENNINES.

S soon as Hannibal was notified in the morning that Scipio and his forces had left their ground, he pressed on after them, eager to overtake them before they could reach the river. But he was too late. The main body of the Roman army had gotten over. There was, however, a detachment of a few hundred men, who had been left on Hannibal's side of the river to guard the bridge until all the army could pass, and then to help in cutting it away. They had accomplished this before Hannibal's arrival but had not had time to make any way to get across the river themselves. Hannibal took them all prisoners.

The condition and prospects of both the Roman and Carthaginian cause were entirely changed by this battle and the retreat of Scipio across the Po. All the nations of the north of Italy, who had been subjects or allies of the Romans, now turned to Hannibal. They sent delegations into his camp, offering him their friendship and alliance.

In fact, a large body of Gauls in the Roman camp, who were fighting under Scipio at the battle of Ticinus, deserted his unit immediately afterward and came over in a mass to Hannibal. They made this revolt in the night, and instead of stealing away secretly, they raised an impressive commotion, killed the guards, filled the camp with their shouts and outcries, and created for a time an awful scene of terror.

Hannibal received them, but he was too wise to admit such a treacherous horde into his army. He treated them with great consideration and kindness and dismissed them to their respective homes with presents, charging them to exert their influence in his favor among the tribes to which they belonged.

Hannibal's soldiers, too, were very much encouraged by the start they had made. The army made immediate preparations for crossing the river. Some of the soldiers built rafts, others went up the stream in search of places to cross on foot. Some swam across. They could adopt these or any other methods in safety, for the Romans made no stand on the opposite bank to oppose them but moved rapidly on, as fast as Scipio could be carried. His wounds began to inflame and were extremely painful.

In fact, the Romans were dismayed at the danger which now threatened them. As soon as news of these events reached the city, the authorities there sent a dispatch to Sicily to recall the other consul. His name was Sempronius. It will be recollected that, when the lots were cast between him and Scipio, it fell to Scipio to proceed to Spain with a plan to stop Hannibal's march, while Sempronius went to Sicily and Africa. The object of this movement was to threaten and attack the Carthaginians at home, in order to distract their attention and prevent them from sending any fresh forces to aid Hannibal and, perhaps, even to compel them to recall him from Italy to defend their own capital. But now that Hannibal had not only passed the Alps, but had also crossed the Po, and was marching toward Rome—Scipio himself disabled and his army fleeing before him—they were obliged at once to abandon the plan of threatening Carthage. They sent with all dispatch an order to Sempronius to hasten home and assist in the defense of Rome.

Sempronius was a man of a very prompt and impulsive character, with great confidence in his own powers, and very ready for action. He came immediately into Italy, recruited new soldiers for the army, put himself at the head of his forces, and marched northward to join Scipio in the valley of the Po. Scipio was suffering great pain from his wounds and could do little to direct the operations of the army. He had slowly retreated before Hannibal, the fever and pain of his wounds being greatly irritated by the motion of traveling. In this manner he arrived at the Trebia, a small stream flowing northward into the Po. He crossed this stream, and finding that he could not go any further on account of his torturous pain, he halted his army, marked out a camp, built up fortifications around it, and prepared to make a stand. To his great relief, Sempronius soon came up and joined him there.

There were now two generals. Napoleon used to say that one bad commander was better than two good ones, so essential is it to success in all military operations to secure that promptness, confidence, and decision which can only exist where action is directed by one single mind. Sempronius and Scipio disagreed as to the proper course to be pursued. Sempronius wished to attack Hannibal immediately. Scipio was in favor of delay. Sempronius attributed Scipio's reluctance to give battle to the dejection of mind and discouragement produced by his wound or to a feeling of envy lest he, Sempronius, should have the honor of conquering the Carthaginians, while he was helpless in his tent. On the other hand, Scipio thought Sempronius inconsiderate and reckless and inclined to rush heedlessly into a battle with a foe whose powers and resources he did not understand.

In the meantime, while the two commanders were divided in opinion, some skirmishes and small conflicts took place between detachments from the two armies, in which Sempronius thought that the Romans had the advantage. This excited his enthusiasm more and more, and he became extremely desirous to bring on a general battle. He began to lose patience with Scipio's caution and delay. The soldiers, he said, were full of strength and courage, all eager for the combat, and it was absurd to hold them back on account of the feebleness of one sick man. "Besides," said he, "of what use can it be to delay any longer? We are as ready to meet the Carthaginians now as we shall ever be. There is no third consul to come and help us; and what a disgrace it is for us Romans, who in the former war led our troops to the very gates of Carthage, to allow Hannibal to have power over all the north of Italy, while we retreat gradually before him, afraid to encounter now a force that we have always conquered before."

Hannibal was not long in learning, through his spies, that there was this difference of opinion between the Roman generals and that Sempronius was full of a presumptuous sort of fervor, and he began to think that he could come up with a plan to draw the latter out into battle under circumstances in which he would have to act at a great disadvantage. He did come up with such a plan. It succeeded admirably; and the case was one of those numerous instances of Hannibal's successful scheming, which led the Romans to say that his leading traits of character were treachery and cunning.

Hannibal's plan was, in a word, an attempt to draw the Roman army out of its camp on a dark, cold, and stormy night and get them into the river Trebia, which flowed between the Roman and Carthaginian camps. His scheme, in detail, was to send a part of his army over the river to attack the Romans in the night or very early in the morning. He hoped that by this means Sempronius would be persuaded to come out of his camp to attack the Carthaginians. The Carthaginians were then to flee and cross the river, and Hannibal hoped that Sempronius would follow, excited by the ardor of pursuit. Hannibal was then to have a strong reserve of the army, that had remained all the time in warmth and safety, to come out and attack the Romans with strength and vigor, while the Romans themselves would be numbed by the cold and wet and disorganized by the confusion produced in crossing the stream.

A part of Hannibal's reserve was to lie in wait to ambush. There were some meadows near the water, which were covered in many places with tall grass and bushes. Hannibal went to examine the spot and found that the shrubbery was high enough for even horsemen to be concealed in it. He placed a thousand foot soldiers and a thousand horsemen here, the most efficient and courageous in the army. He selected them in the following manner:

He called one of his lieutenant generals to the spot, explained his plan to him, and then asked him to go and choose from the cavalry and the infantry, a hundred each, the best soldiers he could find. The two hundred were then assembled, and Hannibal, after surveying them with looks of approval and pleasure, said, "Yes, you are the men I want, only, instead of two hundred, I need two thousand. Go back to the army, and select and bring to me, each of you, nine men like yourselves." It is easy to be imagined that the soldiers were pleased with this commission and that they executed it faithfully. The whole force chosen in this way was soon assembled and stationed in the thickets as described, where they lay in ambush ready to attack the Romans after they crossed the river.

Hannibal also made arrangements for leaving a large part of his army in his own camp, ready for battle, with orders that they should partake of food and refreshments and keep themselves warm by the fires until they were called on. All things being ready, he detached a body of horsemen to cross the river and see if they could provoke the Romans to come out of their camp and pursue them.

"Go," said Hannibal, to the commander of this detachment, "pass the stream, advance to the Roman camp, attack the guards, and when the army forms and comes out to attack you, retreat slowly back across the river."

The detachment did as it was ordered to do. When they arrived at the camp, which was soon after break of day— for it was a part of Hannibal's plan to bring the Romans out before they had time to eat breakfast—Sempronius, at the first alarm, called all the soldiers to arms, supposing that the whole Carthaginian force was attacking them. It was a cold and stormy morning, and the atmosphere was filled with rain and snow, but little else could be seen. Column after column of horsemen and infantry marched out of the camp. The Carthaginians retreated. Sempronius was greatly excited at the idea of so easily driving back the assailants, and as they retreated, he pressed on in pursuit of them. As Hannibal had anticipated, he became so excited in the pursuit that he did not stop at the banks of the river. The Carthaginian horsemen plunged into the stream in their retreat, and the Romans, foot soldiers and horsemen together, followed on. The stream was usually small, but it was now swelled by the rain which had been falling all the night. The water was intensely cold. The Roman horsemen got through tolerably well, but the foot soldiers were all thoroughly drenched and numbed by the cold; and as they had not taken any food that morning and had come forward on a very sudden call, without any sufficient preparation, they felt the effects of the exposure in the strongest degree. Still they pressed on. They ascended the bank after crossing the river, and when they had formed again there and were moving forward in pursuit of their still fleeing enemy, suddenly the whole force of Hannibal's reserves, strong and vigorous, just from their tent and their fires, burst upon them. The Roman soldiers had scarcely recovered from the astonishment and the shock of this unexpected onset, when the two thousand concealed in ambush came rushing forward in the storm and attacked the Romans in the rear with frightful shouts and outcries.

All these movements took place very rapidly. Only a very short period elapsed from the time that the Roman army, officers and soldiers, were quietly sleeping in their camp or rising slowly to prepare for the routine of an ordinary day, before they found themselves all drawn out in battle lines some miles from their camp, surrounded and hemmed in by their foes. The events succeeded each other so rapidly as to appear to the soldiers like a dream; but very soon their wet and freezing clothes, their limbs numb and stiffened, the sleet which was driving along the plain, the endless lines of Carthaginian infantry, hemming them in on all sides, and the columns of horsemen and of elephants charging in on them, convinced them that their situation was one of dreadful reality. The calamity which threatened them was of such a vast extent, as well as imminent and terrible; for, though the scheme of Hannibal was very simple in its plan and management, he had executed it on a great scale and had brought out the whole Roman army. There were, it is said, about forty thousand who crossed the river and about an equal number in the Carthaginian army to oppose them. Such a body of combatants covered a large extent of ground, and the conflict that ensued was one of the most horrible scenes of the many that Hannibal engineered.

The battle continued for many hours, the Romans becoming more and more confused all the time. The elephants of the Carthaginians, the few that now remained, made great havoc in their ranks, and finally, after a battle of some hours, the whole Roman army broke up and fled, some in small units, as their officers could keep them together, and others in hopeless confusion. They made their way back to the river, which they reached at various points up and down the stream. In the meantime, the continued rain had swollen the waters still more—the low lands were flooded, the deep places concealed, and the broad expanse of water in the center of the stream whirled in boiling and muddy currents, whose surface was roughened by the breeze and dotted everywhere with the drops of rain still falling.

When the Roman army was thoroughly broken up and scattered, the Carthaginians gave up any further act of battle. They were too wet, cold, and exhausted themselves to feel any eagerness in the pursuit of their enemies. Vast numbers of the Romans, however, attempted to cross the river and were swept down and destroyed by the merciless flood, whose force they had not enough remaining strength to withstand. Other portions of the troops lay hidden in the places to which they had retreated, until night came on, and then they made rafts on which they planned to float themselves back across the stream. Hannibal's troops were too wet and cold and exhausted to go out again into the storm, and so they did not stop these attempts. However, great numbers of the Roman troops were carried down the stream and lost.

It was now December, too late for Hannibal to attempt to advance much farther that season, and yet the way before him was open to the Apennines, by the defeat of Sempronius, for neither he nor Scipio could now hope to make another stand against him until they could receive new reinforcements from Rome. During the winter months, Hannibal had various battles and adventures, sometimes with portions and detachments of the Roman army and sometimes with the native tribes. He was, at times, in great difficulty for want of food for his army, until at last he bribed the governor of a castle, where a Roman granary was kept, to deliver it up to him, and after that he was well supplied.

The natives of the country were not at all favorable toward him, and in the course of the winter they attempted to obstruct his plans and harass his army by every means in their power. Finding his situation uncomfortable, he moved on toward the south and at eventually decided that, as bad as the season was, he would cross the Apennines.

The great valley of the Po extends across the whole north of Italy. The valley of the Arno and of the Umbro lies south of it, separated from it by a part of the Apennine chain. This southern valley was Etruria. Hannibal decided to attempt to pass over the mountains into Etruria. He thought he would find there a warmer climate and inhabitants more favorable to him, in addition to being so much nearer to Rome.

But, although Hannibal had conquered the Alps, the Apennines conquered him. A very violent storm arose just as he reached the most exposed place among the mountains. It was intensely cold, and the wind blew the hail and snow directly into the faces of the troops, so that it was impossible for them to proceed. They halted and turned their backs to the storm, but the wind increased more and more and was accompanied by terrific thunder and lightning, which filled the soldiers with alarm, as they were at such an altitude as to be themselves enveloped in the clouds from which the peals and flashes were emitted. Unwilling to retreat, Hannibal ordered the army to camp on the spot, in the best shelter they could find. They attempted to pitch their tents, but it was impossible to secure them. The wind increased to a hurricane. The tent poles were unmanageable, and the canvas was carried away from its fastenings and sometimes split or blown into rags by its flapping in the wind. The poor elephants that were left sank down under this intense cold and died. One only remained alive.

Hannibal ordered a retreat, and the army went back into the valley of the Po. But Hannibal was ill at ease here. The natives of the country were very weary of his presence. His army consumed their food, ravaged their country, and destroyed all their peace and happiness. Hannibal suspected them of a plan to poison him or assassinate him in some other way. He was continually watching and taking precautions against these attempts. He had a great many different outfits made to be used as disguises, and false hair of different colors and fashion, so that he could alter his appearance at will. This was to prevent any spy or assassin who might come into his camp from identifying him by any description of his clothing and appearance. Notwithstanding these precautions, he was ill at ease, and at the very earliest opportunity in the spring he made a new attempt to cross the mountains and was successful.

On descending the southern slopes of the Apennines, he learned that a new Roman army, under a new consul, was advancing toward him from the south. He was eager to meet this force and was preparing to press forward by the nearest way. He found, however, that this would lead him across the lower part of the valley of the Arno, which was very broad and, though usually passable, was overflowing due to the melting of the snows upon the mountains. The whole country was now, in fact, a vast expanse of marshes and swamplands.

Still, Hannibal decided to cross it, and in the attempt, he involved his army in difficulties and dangers as great, almost, as he had encountered upon the Alps. The waters were rising continually; they filled all the channels and spread over extended plains. They were so muddy that everything beneath the surface was concealed, and the soldiers wading in them were continually sinking into deep and sudden channels and bogs of mire, where many were lost. They were all exhausted and worn out by the wet and cold and the long exposure to it. They were four days and three nights in this situation, as their progress was, of course, extremely slow. The men, during all this time, had scarcely any sleep, and in some places the only way they could get any rest was to lay their arms and their baggage in the standing water, so as to build, by this means, a sort of couch or platform on which they could lie. Hannibal became sick too. He was attacked with a violent inflammation of the eyes, and eventually he went blind in one of them. He was not, however, so much exposed as the other officers; for there was one elephant left of all those that had began the march in Spain, and Hannibal rode this elephant during the four day march through the water. There were guides and attendants to precede him, for the purpose of finding a safe and practical road, and by their assistance, with the help of the animal's discernment, he got safely through.

CHAPTER VIII

THE DICTATOR FABIUS.

N the meantime, while Hannibal was rapidly making his way toward the gates of Rome, the people of the city became more and more alarmed, until at last a general feeling or terror pervaded all the ranks of society. Citizens and soldiers were struck with one common dread. They had raised a new army and put it under the command of a new consul, for the terms of service of the others had expired. Flaminius was the name of this new commander, and he was moving northward at the head of his forces at the time that Hannibal was moving his troops with so much labor and difficulty through the meadows and morasses of the Arno.

This army was, however, no more successful than its predecessors had been. Hannibal planned to trap Flaminius by a clever scheme, as he had entrapped Sempronius before. There is in the eastern part of Etruria, near the mountains, a lake called Lake Thrasymene. It happened that this lake extended so near to the base of the mountains as to leave only a narrow passage between—a passage just a little wider than was necessary for a road. Hannibal planned to station a detachment of his troops to lie in ambush at the foot of the mountains and others on the cliffs above and then in some way entice Flaminius and his army through the pass. Flaminius was, like Sempronius, ardent, self-confident, and vain. He despised the power of Hannibal and thought that his success to that point had been owing to the inefficiency or indecision of his predecessors. For his part, his only desire was to encounter him, for he was sure of an easy victory. He advanced, therefore, boldly and without concern into the pass of Thrasymene, when he learned that Hannibal was camped beyond it.

Hannibal had established a camp openly on some elevated ground beyond the pass, and as Flaminius and his troops came into the narrowest part of the pass, they saw this camp at a distance before them, with a broad plain beyond the pass between them. They supposed that the whole force of the enemy was there, not dreaming of the presence of the strong detachments which were hidden on the slopes of the mountains above them, and were looking down on them at that very moment from behind rocks and bushes. When the Romans had gotten through the pass, they spread out on the plain beyond it and were advancing to the camp, when suddenly the concealed troops burst forth from their hiding place and, pouring down the mountains, took complete possession of the pass and attacked the Romans in the rear, while Hannibal attacked their front division. Another long, and desperate, and bloody battle ensued. The Romans were beaten at every point, and as they were hemmed in between the lake, the mountain, and the pass, they could not retreat; the army was almost totally cut to pieces. Flaminius was killed.

The news of this battle spread everywhere and produced the strongest sensation. Hannibal sent messages to
Carthage announcing what he considered his final victory
over the great foe, and the news was received with the
greatest rejoicings. At Rome, on the other hand, the news
produced a dreadful shock of disappointment and terror. It
seemed as if the last hope of resisting the progress of their
terrible enemy was gone and that they had nothing now to
do but to sink down in despair and await the hour when
his columns would come pouring in through the gates of
the city.

The people of Rome were, in fact, prepared for a panic,
for their fears had been increasing and gathering strength
for some time. They were very superstitious in those ancient
days in respect to signs and omens. A thousand unimport-
ant occurrences, which would be considered of no consequence whatever in the present day, were then considered
bad signs, predicting terrible calamities; and on occasions like these, when calamities seemed to be impending,
everything was noticed, and circumstances which would
not have been regarded at all in ordinary times were reported from one to another, the stories being exaggerated
as they spread, until the imaginations of the people were
filled with mysterious but invincible fears. So universal was
the belief in these signs and omens that they were sometimes formally reported to the senate, committees were
appointed to inquire into them, and solemn sacrifices were
offered to "make amends for them," that is, to avert the
displeasure of the gods, which the omens were supposed
to foreshadow.

A very curious list of these omens was reported to the
senate during the winter and spring in which Hannibal
was advancing toward Rome. An ox from the cattle market

had gotten into a house and, losing his way, had climbed up into the third story and, being frightened by the noise and uproar of those who followed him, ran out of a window and fell down to the ground. A light appeared in the sky in the form of ships. A temple was struck with lightning. A spear in the hand of a statue of Juno, a celebrated goddess, shook one day, of itself. Ghosts of men in white garments were seen in a certain place. A wolf came into a camp, snatched the sword of a soldier on guard out of his hands and ran away with it. The sun one day looked smaller than usual. Two moons were seen together in the sky. This was in the daytime, and one of the moons was doubtless a halo or a white cloud. Stones fell out of the sky at a place called Picenum. This was one of the most dreadful of all the omens, though the falling of these meteorites is now known to be a common occurrence.

These omens were all real occurrences, more or less remarkable, but meant nothing in respect to their being indications of impending calamities. Other things were reported to the senate which must have originated almost totally in the imaginations and fears of the observers. Two shields, it was said, in a certain camp, sweat blood. Some people were reaping, and bloody ears of grain fell into the basket. This must have been totally imaginary, unless one of the reapers had cut his fingers with the sickle. Some streams and fountains became bloody; and finally, in one place in the country, some goats turned into sheep. Also, a hen became a rooster, and a rooster changed to a hen.

Such ridiculous stories would not be worthy of a moment's attention now were it not for the degree of importance attached to them then. They were formally reported to the Roman senate, the witnesses who asserted that they had seen them were called in and examined, and a solemn debate was held on the question what should be done to avert the supernatural influences of evil which the omens expressed. The senate decided to have three days to make amends and sacrifice, during which all the people of Rome devoted themselves to the religious observances which they thought would be suitable to appease the wrath of Heaven. They made various offerings and gifts to the different gods, among which one was a golden thunderbolt of fifty pounds' weight, manufactured for Jupiter, whom they considered the thunderer.

All these things took place before the battle at Lake Thrasymene, so that the whole community was in a very feverish state of excitement and anxiety before the news from Flaminius arrived. When the news at last came, it threw the whole city into utter terror. Of course, the messenger went directly to the senate house to report to the government, but the story that such news had arrived soon spread about the city, and the whole population crowded into the streets and public squares eagerly asking for the news. An enormous crowd assembled before the senate house calling for information. A public officer appeared at last and said to them in a loud voice, "We have been defeated in a great battle." He would say no more. Still, rumors spread from one to another, until it was generally known throughout the city that Hannibal had conquered the Roman army again in a great battle, that great numbers of the soldiers had fallen or been taken prisoners, and that the consul himself was slain.

The night was passed in great anxiety and terror, and the next day, and for several of the succeeding days, the people gathered in great numbers around the gates, inquiring eagerly for news of everyone that came in from the country. Eventually, scattered soldiers and small bodies of troops began to arrive, bringing with them information of the battle, each one having a different tale to tell, according to his own individual experience in the scene. Whenever these men arrived, the people of the city, and especially the women who had husbands or sons in the army, crowded around them, overwhelming them with questions and making them tell their tale again and again, as if the intolerable suspense and anxiety of the hearers could not be satisfied. The news confirmed and increased the fears of those who listened to it; but sometimes, when it made known the safety of a husband or a son, it produced as much relief and rejoicing as it did in other cases terror and despair. That maternal love was as strong an impulse in those rough days as it is in the more refined and cultivated periods of the present age is evident by the fact that two of these Roman mothers, on seeing their sons coming suddenly into their presence, alive and well, when they had heard that they had fallen in battle, were killed at once by the shock of surprise and joy, as if by a blow.

In seasons of great and imminent danger to the commonwealth, it was the custom of the Romans to appoint what they called a dictator, that is, a supreme executive, who was clothed with absolute and unlimited powers; and the responsibility was on him to save the state from the threatened ruin by the most prompt action. This was obviously one of the emergencies requiring such a measure. There was no time for deliberations and debates; for deliberations and debates, in periods of such excitement and danger, become disputes and end in tumult and uproar. Hannibal was at the head of a victorious army, ravaging the country which he had already conquered, with no obstacle between him and the city itself. It was an emergency calling for the appointment of a dictator. The people chose a man of great reputation for experience and wisdom named Fabius and placed the whole power of the state in his hands. All other authority was suspended, and everything was subjected to his power. The whole city, with the life and property of every inhabitant, was placed at his disposal; the army and the fleets were also under his command; even the consuls were subject to his orders.

Fabius accepted the vast responsibility which his election imposed upon him and immediately began to take the necessary measures. He first made arrangements for performing solemn religious ceremonies to make amends for the omens and calm the gods. He brought out all the people in great assemblies and made them take vows in the most formal and imposing manner, promising offerings and celebrations in honor of the various gods, at some future time, should the gods avert the threatening danger. It is doubtful, however, whether Fabius, in doing these things, really believed that they had any actual effect or whether he resorted to them as a means of calming and quieting the minds of the people and producing that composure and confidence which always results from a hope of the favor of Heaven. If this last was his object, his conduct was truly wise.

Fabius, also, immediately ordered a large drafting of troops to be made. His second in command, called his *master of horse,* was directed to make the draft and to assemble the troops at a place called Tibur, a few miles east of the city. There was always a master of horse appointed to attend to and second a dictator. The name of this officer in the case of Fabius was Minucius. Minucius was as ardent, prompt, and impetuous as Fabius was cool, prudent and calculating. He collected the troops and brought them to their place of rendezvous. Fabius went out to take command of them. One of the consuls was coming to join him with a body of troops which he had under his command. Fabius sent word to him that he must come without any of the insignia of his authority, as all his authority, semi-regal as it was in ordinary times, was superseded and overruled in the presence of a dictator. A consul was accustomed to move in great style and manner on all occasions. He was preceded by twelve men, bearing badges and insignia, to impress the army and the people with a sense of the greatness of his dignity. To see, therefore, a consul divested of all these marks of his power, and coming into the dictator's presence as any other officer would come before an acknowledged superior, made the army of Fabius feel a very strong sense of the greatness of their new commander's dignity and power.

Fabius then issued a proclamation, which he sent by proper messengers into all the regions of the country around Rome, especially to that part toward the territory which Hannibal possessed. In this proclamation he ordered all the people to abandon the country and the towns which were not strongly fortified and to seek shelter in the castles, forts, and fortified cities. They were also commanded to lay waste the country which they would leave, and destroy all the property, and especially all the provisions, which they could not take to their places of refuge. This being done, Fabius placed himself at the head of the forces which he had called together and moved on with great caution, in search of his enemy.

In the meantime, Hannibal had crossed over to the eastern side of Italy and passed down, conquering and ravaging the country as he went, until he got considerably south of Rome. He seemed to have thought it not quite prudent to advance to the actual attack of the city,

after the battle of Lake Thrasymene; for the vast population of Rome was sufficient, if rendered desperate by his
actually threatening the capture and pillage of the city, to
overwhelm his army entirely. So he moved to the east and
advanced on that side until he had passed the city, and so
it happened that Fabius had to march to the south and east
in order to meet him. The two armies came in sight of each
other on the eastern side of Italy, very near the shores of
the Adriatic Sea.

The policy which Fabius adopted was not to give Hannibal battle but to watch him and wear his army out by
fatigue and delays. He kept near him but always posted
his army on ground that provided an advantage, which all
the defiance and provoking of Hannibal could not induce
him to leave. When Hannibal moved, which he was soon
compelled to do to obtain provisions, Fabius would move
too but only to post and position himself in some place of
security as before. Hannibal did everything in his power to
bring Fabius to battle, but all his efforts were futile.

In fact, he was at one time in imminent danger. He had
been drawn, by Fabius's good skill, into a place where he
was surrounded by mountains, on which Fabius had posted
his troops, and there was only one passage which offered
any exit, and this, too, Fabius had strongly guarded. Hannibal resorted to his usual resource, cunning and scheming, for means of escape. He collected a herd of oxen. He
tied twigs across their horns, filling the twigs with tar, so
as to make them highly combustible. In the night on which
he was going to attempt to proceed through the pass, he
ordered his army to be ready to march through and then
had the oxen driven up the hills around on the further side
of the Roman detachment which was guarding the pass.
The twigs were then lit on the horns of the oxen. They ran

about, frightened and infuriated by the fire, which burned their horns to the quick and blinded them with the sparks which fell from it. The leaves and branches of the forests were set on fire. A great commotion was thus made, and the guards, seeing the moving lights and hearing the tumult, supposed that the Carthaginian army was on the heights and coming down to attack them. They turned out in great hurry and confusion to meet the imaginary foe, leaving the pass unguarded and, while they were pursuing the bonfires on the oxen's heads into all sorts of dangerous and impractical places, Hannibal quietly marched his army through the pass and reached a place of safety.

Although Fabius kept Hannibal busy and prevented him from approaching the city, there soon began to be a considerable degree of dissatisfaction that Fabius did not act more decidedly. Minucius was continually urging him to give Hannibal battle, and not being able to induce him to do so, he was continually expressing his discontent and displeasure. The army sympathized with Minucius. He wrote home to Rome too, complaining bitterly of the dictator's inefficiency. Hannibal learned all this by means of his spies, and other sources of information, which schemers always have at command. Hannibal was, of course, very pleased to hear of these disagreements, and of the unpopularity of Fabius. He considered such an enemy as Fabius—so prudent, cautious and watchful—as a far more dangerous foe than such bold and impetuous commanders as Flaminius and Minucius, whom he could always entice into difficulty and then easily conquer.

Hannibal thought he would give Minucius a little help in making Fabius unpopular. He found out from Roman deserters that the dictator possessed a valuable farm in the country, and he sent a detachment of his troops there, with orders to plunder and destroy the property all around it but to leave the farm of Fabius untouched and in safety. The object was to give the enemies of Fabius at Rome a reason to say that there was secretly a good understanding between him and Hannibal and that he was kept back from acting boldly in defense of his country by some corrupt bargain which he had traitorously made with the enemy.

The plan succeeded. Discontent and dissatisfaction spread rapidly, both in the camp and in the city. At Rome they made an urgent demand for Fabius to return on the pretense that they wanted him to take part in some religious ceremonies, but really to remove him from the camp, and give Minucius an opportunity to attack Hannibal. They also wanted to devise some method, if possible, of depriving him of his power. He had been appointed for six months, and the time had not yet nearly expired; but they wished to shorten or, if they could not shorten, to limit and diminish his power.

Fabius went to Rome, leaving the army under the orders of Minucius but commanding him under no circumstances to give Hannibal battle nor to expose his troops to any danger but to pursue steadily the same policy which he had followed. He had, however, been in Rome only a short time before news came that Minucius had fought a battle and gained a victory. Minucius sent boastful and exaggerated letters to the Roman senate, lauding the exploit which he had performed.

Fabius carefully examined the accounts. He compared one thing with another and satisfied himself of what afterward proved to be the truth—Minucius had gained no victory at all. He had lost five or six thousand men, and Hannibal had lost no more. Fabius showed that no advantage had been gained. He urged the senate to understand the importance of adhering to the line of policy he had pursued, and the danger of risking everything, as Minucius had done, on the fortunes of a single battle. Besides, he said, Minucius had disobeyed his orders, which were distinct and positive, and he deserved to be recalled.

In saying these things Fabius irritated and exasperated his enemies more than ever. "Here is a man," said they, "who will not fight the enemies whom he is sent against, and he will also not allow anybody else to fight them. Even at this distance, when his second in command has obtained a victory, he will not admit it, and attempts to diminish the advantages of it. He wishes to prolong the war, that he may the longer continue to enjoy the supreme and unlimited authority with which we have entrusted him."

The hostility towards Fabius at last reached such a pitch that it was proposed in an assembly of the people to make Minucius his equal in command. Fabius, having finished the business which called him to Rome, did not wait to attend to the discussion of this question but left the city and was proceeding on his way to join the army again, when he was overtaken with a messenger bearing a letter informing him that the decree had passed and that he must from then on consider Minucius as his colleague and equal. Minucius was, of course, extremely elated at this result. "Now," he said, "we will see if something can be done."

The first question was to decide on what principle and in what way they should share their power. "We cannot both command at once," said Minucius. "Let us exercise the power in alternation, each one being in authority for a day, a week, a month, or any other period that you prefer."

"No," replied Fabius, "we will not divide the time, we will divide the men. There are four legions. You shall take two of them, and the other two shall be mine. I can, perhaps, save half the army from the dangers in which I fear your impulsiveness will plunge all whom you have under your command."

This plan was adopted. The army was divided, and each portion went, under its own leader, to its separate camps. The result was one of the most strange and extraordinary occurrences that is recorded in the history of nations.

Hannibal, who was well informed of all these transactions, immediately felt that Minucius was in his power. He knew that he was so eager for battle that it would be easy to entice him into it, under almost any circumstances that he might choose to arrange. Accordingly, he waited for an opportunity when there was a good place for an ambush near Minucius's camp, and lodged five thousand men in it in such a manner that they were concealed by rocks and other obstructions to the view. There was a hill between this ground and the camp of Minucius. When the ambush was ready, Hannibal sent up a small force to take possession of the top of the hill anticipating that Minucius would at once send up a stronger force to drive them away. He did so. Hannibal then sent up more as reinforcements. Minucius, whose spirit and pride were now stirred, sent up more still, and thus, by degrees, Hannibal drew out his enemy's whole force and then ordered his own troops to retreat before them. The Romans were drawn down the hill until they were surrounded by the ambush. The hidden troops came pouring down on them, and in a short time the Romans were thrown into utter confusion, flying in all directions before their enemies and entirely at their mercy.

All would have been irretrievably lost had it not been for the intervention of Fabius. He received news of the danger at his own camp and marched out at once with all his force. He arrived at the appropriate time and acted so efficiently that he at once completely changed the fate of the day. He saved Minucius and his half of the army from utter destruction. The Carthaginians retreated, Hannibal being entirely overwhelmed with disappointment and irritation at being deprived of his prey. History relates that Minucius had the sincerity and good sense, after this, to acknowledge his error and to yield to the guidance and direction of Fabius. He called his part of the army together when they reached their camp and addressed them with this: "Fellow soldiers, I have often heard it said that the wisest men are those who possess wisdom and discernment themselves and, next to them, those who know how to recognize and are willing to be guided by the wisdom and discernment of others; while they are fools who do not know how to manage themselves and will not be guided by those who do. We will not belong to this last class; and since it is proved that we are not entitled to stand with the first, let us join the second. We will march to the camp of Fabius and join our camp with his, as before. We owe to him, and also to all his portion of the army, our eternal gratitude for the nobleness of spirit which he manifested in coming to our deliverance, when he might so justly have left us to ourselves."

The two legions went to the camp of Fabius, and a complete and permanent reconciliation took place between the two divisions of the army. Fabius rose very high in the general esteem by this action. The term of his dictatorship, however, expired soon after this, and as the danger from Hannibal was now less imminent, the office was not renewed, but consuls were chosen as before.

The character of Fabius has been regarded with the highest admiration by all mankind. He displayed a very noble spirit in all that he did. One of his last acts was a very striking proof of this. He had bargained with Hannibal to pay a certain sum of money as ransom for a number of prisoners which had fallen into his hands, and whom Hannibal, on the faith of that promise, had released. Fabius believed that the Romans would readily ratify the treaty and pay the amount; but they objected, being displeased, or pretending to be displeased, because Fabius had not consulted them before making the arrangement. Fabius, in order to preserve his own and his country's faith unsullied, sold his farm to raise the money. He did this most certainly to protect and vindicate his own honor, but he can hardly be said to have saved that of the people of Rome.

CHAPTER IX

THE BATTLE OF CANNAE.

HE battle of Cannae was the last great battle fought by Hannibal in Italy. This conflict has been greatly celebrated in history, not only for its magnitude and the terrible desperation with which it was fought but also on account of the strong interest which the circumstances surrounding it excited. This interest is perhaps due more to the peculiar skill of the ancient historians who narrate the story, rather than the events which are recorded.

It was about a year after the close of the dictatorship of Fabius that this battle was fought. That interval had been spent by the Roman consuls who were in office during that time in various military operations, which did not, however, lead to any decisive results. In the meantime, there was great uneasiness, discontent, and dissatisfaction in Rome. To have such a dangerous and terrible foe at the head of forty thousand men, infesting the regions near their city, ravaging the territories of their friends and allies, and threatening continually to attack the city itself, was a continual source of anxiety and frustration. It mortified the Roman pride, too, to find that the greatest armies they could raise and the most capable generals they could choose and commission proved totally unable to cope with the foe. The cleverest of them had felt it necessary to decline the contest with Hannibal altogether.

This state of things produced a great deal of ill humor in the city. Party spirit ran very high; tumultuous assemblies were held; disputes and arguments prevailed; and mutual charges and countercharges were exchanged without end. There were two great parties formed: that of the moderate classes on one side and the aristocracy on the other. The former was called the Plebeians, the latter the Patricians. The division between these two classes was very great and very strongly marked. There was, as a result, great difficulty in the election of consuls. At last the consuls were chosen, one from each party. The name of the Patrician was Paulus Aemilius. The name of the Plebeian was Varro. They were inducted into office and put jointly into possession of a vast power. To wield such power with any efficiency and success would seem to require unity and harmony in those who held it, and yet Aemilius and Varro were confirmed and unbending political foes. It was often so in the Roman government. The consulship was a double-headed monster, which spent half its strength in bitter contests waged between its members.

The Romans decided to make an effective effort to rid themselves of their foe. They raised an enormous army. It consisted of eight legions. The Roman legion was an army of itself. It normally contained four thousand foot soldiers and a troop of three hundred horsemen. It was very unusual to have more than two or three legions in the field at a time. The Romans, however, on this occasion, increased the number of the legions and also increased their size, so that they contained, each, five thousand infantry and four hundred cavalry. They were determined to make a great and last effort to defend their city and save the common-wealth from ruin. Aemilius and Varro prepared to take command of this great force, with a strong determination to make it the means of Hannibal's destruction.

The characters of the two commanders, however, as well as their political connections, were very dissimilar, and they soon began to manifest a very different spirit and to assume a very different air and bearing from each other. Aemilius was a friend of Fabius and approved of his policy. Varro was for faster action and decision. He made great promises and spoke with the utmost confidence of being able to annihilate Hannibal at a blow. He condemned the policy of Fabius in attempting to wear out the enemy by delays. He said it was a plan of the aristocratic party to protract the war, in order to put themselves in high offices and perpetuate their importance and influence. He said, the war should have been ended long ago and he promised the people that he would now end it, without fail, the very day that he came in sight of Hannibal.

As for Aemilius, he assumed a very different tone. He was surprised, he said, that any man could pretend to decide before he had even left the city how soon and under what circumstances it would be wise to give battle. Plans must be formed to adapt to circumstances, as cir-cumstances cannot be altered to suit plans. He believed that they would succeed in the battle with Hannibal, but he thought that their only hope of success must be based on the exercise of discretion, caution, and discernment; he was sure that rashness and folly could only lead in the future, as they had always done in the past, to embarrass-ment and ruin.

It is said that Fabius, the former dictator, conversed with Aemilius before his departure for the army and gave him such counsel as his age and experience and his knowledge of the character and operation of Hannibal suggested to his mind. "If you had a colleague like yourself," said he, "I would not offer you any advice; you would not need it. Or, if you were yourself like your colleague—vain, self-conceited, and presumptuous—then I would be silent; counsel would be thrown away on you. But as it is, while you have great judgment and discernment to guide you, you are to be placed in a situation of extreme difficulty and peril. If I am not mistaken, the greatest difficulty you will have to encounter will not be the open enemy you are going to meet upon the field. You will find, I think, that Varro will give you quite as much trouble as Hannibal. He will be presumptuous, reckless, and headstrong. He will inspire all the rash and ardent young men in the army with his own enthusiastic folly, and we will be very fortunate if we do not see the terrible and bloody scenes of Lake Thrasymene acted again. I am sure that the true policy for us to adopt is the case which I marked out. That is always the proper course for the invaded to pursue with invaders, where there is the least doubt of the success of a battle. We grow strong while Hannibal grows continually weaker by delay. He can only prosper so long as he can fight battles and perform brilliant exploits. If we deprive him of this power, his strength will be continually wasting away and the spirit and courage of his men waning. He has now scarce a third part of the army which he had when he crossed the Iberus, and nothing can save this remnant from destruction if we are wise."

Aemilius said, in reply to this, that he was going into the operation with very little encouragement or hope. If

Fabius had found it so difficult to withstand the turbulent influences of his master of horse, who was his subordinate officer and, as such, under his command, how could *he* expect to restrain his colleague, who was entitled by his office to full equality with him. But, notwithstanding the difficulties which he foresaw, he was going to do his duty and abide by the result; and if the result should be unfavorable, he would seek death in the conflict, for death by Carthaginian spears was a far lighter evil, in his view, than the displeasure and censures of his countrymen.

The consuls departed from Rome to join the army, Aemilius attended by a moderate number of men of rank and station and Varro by a much larger group, though it was formed of people from the lower classes of society. The army was organized, and the arrangements of the camps were perfected. One ceremony was that of administering an oath to the soldiers, as was usual in the Roman armies at the start of a military operation. They were made to swear that they would not desert the army, that they would never abandon the post to which they were stationed in fear or in flight nor leave the ranks except for the purpose of taking up or recovering a weapon, striking an enemy, or protecting a friend. When those and other arrangements were completed, the army was ready for the field. The consuls made a different arrangement in respect to the division of their power from that adopted by Fabius and Flaminius. It was agreed between them that they would exercise their common authority alternately, each for a day.

In the meantime, Hannibal began to have a great difficulty obtaining provisions for his men. The policy of Fabius had been so far successful as to place him in a very embarrassing situation, which was growing more and more embarrassing every day. He could obtain no food except what he got by plunder, and there was now very little opportunity for that, as the inhabitants of the country had carried off all the grain and deposited it in strongly-fortified towns; and though Hannibal had great confidence in his power to cope with the Roman army in a regular battle on an open field, he had not strength sufficient to destroy a fortress or attack fortified camps. His stock of provisions had become, therefore, nearly exhausted. He had a supply for only ten days, and he saw no possible method of increasing it.

His great object was, therefore, to bring on a battle. Varro was ready and willing to give him battle, but Aemilius desired to persevere in the Fabian policy until the ten days had expired, after which he knew that Hannibal would be reduced to extreme distress and might have to surrender to save his army from actual famine. In fact, it was said that the troops were on such small rations as to produce great discontent and that a large body of Spaniards were preparing to desert and go over together to the Roman camp.

Things were in this state, when, one day, Hannibal sent out a party from his camp to obtain food, and Aemilius, who happened to hold the command that day, sent out a strong force to intercept them. He was successful. The Carthaginian detachment was overwhelmingly defeated. Nearly two thousand men were killed, and the rest fled, by any roads they could find, back to Hannibal's camp. Varro was very eager to follow them there, but Aemilius ordered his men to halt. He was afraid of some trick or treachery on the part of Hannibal and was willing to be satisfied with the victory he had already won.

This little success, however, only inflamed Varro's fervor for a battle and produced a general enthusiasm in the Roman army; and a day or two afterward, a situation occurred which raised this excitement to the highest pitch.

Some soldiers, who had been stationed within sight of Hannibal's camp to watch for signs of movement, sent in word to the consuls that the Carthaginian guards around their camp had all suddenly disappeared and an extraordinary and unusual silence reigned within. Parties of the Roman soldiers went up gradually and cautiously to the Carthaginian lines and soon found that the camp was deserted, though the fires were still burning and the tents remained. This news, of course, put the whole Roman army into a fever of excitement and agitation. They crowded around the consuls' pavilions and with a loud outcry insisted on being led on to take possession of the camp and to pursue the enemy. "He has fled," they said, "and with such haste that he has left the tents standing and his fires still burning. Lead us on in pursuit of him."

Varro was as much excited as the rest. He was eager for action. Aemilius hesitated. He said they ought to proceed with caution. Finally, he called on a certain wise and practical officer, named Statilius, and ordered him to take a small body of horsemen, ride over to the Carthaginian camp, determine the facts exactly, and report the result. Statilius did so. When he reached the lines he ordered his troops to halt and took with him two horsemen on whose courage and strength he could rely and rode in. The three horsemen rode around the camp and examined everything with a view of determining whether Hannibal had really abandoned his position and fled or whether some scheme was intended.

When he came back he reported to the army that, in his opinion, the desertion of the camp was not real but a trick to draw the Romans into some difficulty. The fires were the largest on the side toward the Romans, which indicated that they were built to deceive. He saw money, too, and other valuables strewed about upon the ground, which appeared to him much more like a bait set in a trap than like property abandoned by fugitives as burdens to flight. Varro was not convinced; and the army, hearing of the money, was excited to a greater eagerness for plunder. They could hardly be restrained. Just then, however, two slaves that had been taken prisoners by the Carthaginians some time before came into the Roman camp. They told the consuls that the whole Carthaginian force was hidden in ambush very near, waiting for the Romans to enter their camp, when they were going to surround them and cut them to pieces. In the bustle and movement accompanying on this plan, the slaves had escaped. Of course, the Roman army was now convinced. They returned, annoyed and disappointed, to their own quarters, and Hannibal, still more annoyed and disappointed, returned to his.

He soon found that he could not remain any longer where he was. His provisions were exhausted, and he could obtain no more. The Romans would not come out of their camps to give him battle on equal terms, and they were too strongly fortified to be attacked where they were. He decided to evacuate that part of the country and move, by a sudden march, into Apulia.

Apulia was on the eastern side of Italy. The River Aufidus runs through it, having a town named Cannae near its mouth. The region of the Aufidus was a warm and sunny valley, which was now waving with ripening grain. Being further south, and more exposed to the influence of the sun, Hannibal thought the crops would ripen sooner, and he would have a new field to plunder.

He was fully decided now to leave his camp and move into Apulia. He made the same arrangements as before, when his departure was a mere pretense. He left tents pitched and fires burning but marched his army off the ground by night and secretly, so that the Romans did not notice his departure; and the next day, when they saw the appearances of silence and solitude about the camp, they suspected another deception and made no move themselves. Finally, the news came that the long columns of Hannibal's army had been seen far to the east and moving on as fast as possible with all their baggage. The Romans, after much debate and uncertainty, decided to follow. The eagles of the Apennines looked down on the two great moving masses, creeping slowly along through the forests and valleys, like swarms of insects, one following the other, led on by a strange but strong attraction, drawing them toward each other when at a distance, but kept apart by a still stronger repulsion when near.

The Roman army caught up with Hannibal on the River Aufidus, near Cannae, and the two vast camps were formed with all the noise and excitement made by the movements of two great armies posting themselves on the eve of a battle. In the Roman camp, the confusion was greatly aggravated by the angry disputes which immediately arose between the consuls and their respective supporters as to the course to be pursued. Varro insisted on giving the Carthaginians immediate battle. Aemilius refused. Varro said that he must protest against the continued inexcusable delays and insist on a battle. He would not consent to be responsible any further for allowing Italy to lie at the mercy of such a scourge. Aemilius replied that if Varro did start a battle, he would protest against his rashness, and could not be, in any degree, responsible for the result. The various officers took sides—some with one consul and some with the other, but most with Varro. The dissension filled the camp with emotion, agitation, and ill will.

In the meantime, the inhabitants of the country into which these two vast hordes of ferocious, though restrained and organized combatants, had made such a sudden disruption, were fleeing as fast as they could from the awful scene which they expected was to ensue. They carried from their villages and cabins what little property could be saved and took the women and children away to retreats and secret places, wherever they imagined they could find temporary concealment or protection. The news of the movement of the two armies spread throughout the country, carried by hundreds of refugees and messengers, and all Italy, looking on with suspense and anxiety, awaited the result.

The armies maneuvered for a day or two: Varro, during his term of command, making arrangements to promote and take action and Aemilius, on the following day, doing everything in his power to prevent it. In the end, Varro succeeded. The lines were formed and the battle would start. Aemilius gave up the contest now, and while he protested earnestly against the course which Varro pursued, he prepared to do all in his power to prevent a defeat, since there was no longer a possibility of avoiding a battle.

The battle began, and the reader must imagine the scene, since no pen can fully describe it. Fifty thousand men on one side and eighty thousand on the other, hard at work and steadily, for six hours, killing each other by every possible means of destruction—stabs, blows, struggles, outcries, shouts of anger and defiance, and screams of terror and agony, all mingled together in one general deafening noise, which covered the whole country for an extent of many miles. All together this constituted a scene of horror, which none but those who have witnessed great battles can imagine.

It seems as if Hannibal could do nothing without strategy. In the early part of this conflict he sent a large body of his troops over to the Romans as deserters. They threw down their spears and bucklers, as they reached the Roman lines, in token of surrender. The Romans received them, opened a passage for them, and ordered them to remain there. As they were apparently unarmed, they left only a very small guard to keep them in custody. The men had, however, daggers concealed under their clothes, and watching for a favorable moment in the midst of the battle, they sprang to their feet, drew out their weapons, broke away from their guard, and attacked the Romans at a moment when they were so pressed by the enemy in front that they could scarcely maintain their ground.

It was evident before many hours that the Roman forces were all yielding. From slowly and reluctantly yielding they soon began to flee. In the flight, the weak and the wounded were trampled underfoot by the crowd pressing in behind them or were dispatched by wanton blows from enemies as they passed in pursuit of those who were still able to flee. In the midst of the scene, a Roman officer named Lentulus, as he was riding away, saw in front of him at the roadside another officer wounded, sitting on a stone, faint and bleeding. He stopped when he reached him and found that it was the consul Aemilius. He had been wounded in the head with a sling, and his strength was almost gone. Lentulus offered him his horse and urged him to take it and flee. Aemilius declined the offer. He said it was too late for his life to be saved and he had no wish to save it. "Go on, therefore, yourself," said he, "as fast as you can. Make the best of your way to Rome. Tell the authorities there, from me, that all is lost, and they must do whatever they can for the defense of the city. Make all the speed you can, or Hannibal will be at the gates before you."

Aemilius sent also a message to Fabius, declaring to him that it was not his fault that a battle had been risked with Hannibal. He had done all in his power, he said, to prevent it and had followed the policy which Fabius had recommended to the last. Lentulus, having received these messages and perceiving that the Carthaginians were closing in on him in pursuit, rode away, leaving the consul to his fate. The Carthaginians came on, and seeing the wounded man, they thrust their spears into his body, one after another, as they passed, until his limbs ceased to quiver. As for the other consul, Varro, he escaped with his life. Attended by about seventy horsemen, he made his way to a fortified town not very far from the battlefield, where he stopped with his horsemen and decided that he would attempt to rally there the remains of the army.

The Carthaginians, when they found the victory complete, abandoned the pursuit of the enemy, returned to their camp, spent some hours in feasting and rejoicing, and then laid down to sleep. They were, of course, well-exhausted by the intense exertions of the day. On the field where the battle had been fought, the wounded lay all night mingled with the dead, filling the air with cries and groans and writhing in agony.

Early the next morning the Carthaginians came back to the field to plunder the dead bodies of the Romans. The whole field presented a most shocking spectacle. The bodies of horses and men lay mingled in dreadful confusion, as they had fallen: some dead, others still alive, the men moaning, crying for water, and feebly struggling from time to time to disentangle themselves from the heaps of carcasses under which they were buried. The deadly and inextinguishable hate which the Carthaginians felt for their foes not having been appeased by the slaughter of forty thousand of them, they beat down and stabbed these wretched lingerers wherever they found them, as a

sort of morning pastime after the more difficult labors of
the preceding day. This slaughter, however, could hardly
be considered a cruelty to the wretched victims of it, for
many of them bared their breasts to their assailants and
begged for the blow which was to put an end to their pain.
In exploring the field, one Carthaginian soldier was found
still alive but imprisoned by the dead body of his Roman
enemy lying upon him. The Carthaginian's face and ears
were shockingly mangled. The Roman, having fallen upon
him when both were mortally wounded, had continued
the combat with his teeth when he could no longer use his
weapon and had died at last, binding down his exhausted
enemy with his own dead body.

The Carthaginians secured a vast amount of plunder.
The Roman army was full of officers and soldiers from the
aristocratic ranks of society, and their arms and their dress
were very valuable. The Carthaginians obtained baskets
of gold rings from their fingers, which Hannibal sent to
Carthage as a trophy of his victory.

CHAPTER X

SCIPIO.

HE true reason why Hannibal could not be arrested in his triumphant career seems not to have been because the Romans did not pursue the right kind of policy toward him but because, thus far, they had no general who was his equal. Whoever was sent against him soon proved to be his inferior. Hannibal outmaneuvered them all in strategy and conquered them on the field. There was, however, now destined to appear a man capable of coping with Hannibal. It was young Scipio, the one who saved the life of his father at the battle of Ticinus, described in chapter six. The son of Hannibal's first great antagonist of that name is commonly called in history, the elder Scipio. But there was yet a third by the name that came after him, who was greatly celebrated for his wars against the Carthaginians in Africa. The last two received, from the Roman people, the surname Africanus, in honor of their African victories. The one now entering the stage was called Scipio Africanus

the elder, or sometimes simply the elder Scipio. The deeds
of the Scipio who attempted to stop Hannibal at the Rhone
and on the Po were so totally eclipsed by his son, and by
the other Scipio who followed him, that the former is left
out of view and forgotten.

Our current Scipio first appears on the stage, in the
exercise of military command, after the battle of Cannae.
He was a subordinate officer. On the day following the
battle he found himself at a place called Canusium, a short
distance from Cannae on the way toward Rome, with a
number of other officers of his own rank, and broken
masses and detachments of the army coming in from time
to time, faint, exhausted, and in despair. The rumor was
that both consuls were killed. These fragments of the army
had, therefore, no one to command them. The officers met
together and unanimously agreed to make Scipio their
commander in the emergency, until some superior officer
should arrive, or they should get orders from Rome.

An incident occurred which showed the boldness and
energy of the young Scipio's character. At the meeting in
which he was placed in command, an officer came in and
reported that in another part of the camp there was an
assembly of officers and young men of rank, headed by a
certain Metellus, who had decided to give up the cause of
their country in despair, and were making arrangements
to proceed immediately to the sea coast, obtain ships, and
sail away to seek a new home in some foreign lands, considering their cause in Italy as utterly lost and ruined. The
officer proposed that they should call a council and deliberate what was best to do.

"Deliberate!" said Scipio; "this is not a case for deliberation, but for action. Draw your swords and follow me."
So saying, he pressed forward at the head of the party to

the quarters of Metellus. They marched boldly into the building where he and his friends were in consultation. Scipio held up his sword and in a very solemn manner pronounced an oath, binding himself not to abandon his country in this the hour of her distress nor to allow any other Roman citizen to abandon her. If he should be guilty of such treason, he called upon Jupiter, by the most dreadful curse, to destroy him utterly, house, family, fortune, soul, and body.

"And now, Metellus, I call upon you," said he, "and all who are with you, to take the same oath. You must do it; otherwise you must defend yourselves against these swords of ours, as well as those of the Carthaginians." Metellus and his party yielded. It was not totally to fear that they yielded. It was to the influence of hope quite as much as to that of fear. The courage, the energy, and the warlike fervor which Scipio's conduct revealed, awakened a similar spirit in them, and made them hope again that possibly their country might yet be saved.

The news of the awful defeat and destruction of the Roman army flew swiftly to Rome and produced universal terror. The whole city was in an uproar. There were soldiers in the army from almost every family, so that every woman and child throughout the city was distracted by the double torment of inconsolable grief at the death of their husband or their father, slain in the battle, and of terrible fear that Hannibal and his raging followers were about to burst in through the gates of the city to murder them. The streets of the city, and especially the Forum, were congested with vast crowds of men, women, and children, who filled the air with loud expressions of grief and with cries of terror and despair.

The magistrates were not able to restore order. The senate actually adjourned so that the members of it might go about the city and use their influence and their power to produce silence at least, if they could not restore composure. The streets were finally cleared. The women and children were ordered to remain at home. Armed patrols were put on guard to prevent riotous assemblies forming. Men were sent off on horseback on the road to Canusium and Cannae to get more accurate information, and then the senate assembled again and began to consider, with as much calmness as they could command, what was to be done.

However, the panic at Rome was in some measure, a false alarm, for Hannibal, contrary to the expectation of all Italy, did not go to Rome. His generals urged him very strongly to do so. Nothing could prevent, they said, his gaining immediate possession of the city. But Hannibal refused to do this. Rome was strongly fortified and had an immense population. His army, too, was much weakened by the battle of Cannae, and he thought it most prudent not to attempt to overtake Rome until he received reinforcements from home. It was now so late in the season that he could not expect such reinforcements immediately, and he therefore decided to select some place more accessible than Rome and make it his headquarters for the winter. He decided in favor of Capua, which was a large and powerful city one or two hundred miles southeast of Rome.

Hannibal, in fact, came up with the plan of retaining possession of Italy and of making Capua the capital of the country, leaving Rome to itself to decline, as under such circumstances it inevitably must, to the rank of a second city. Perhaps he was tired of the fatigues and hazards of war, and having narrowly escaped ruin before the battle of Cannae, he now resolved that he would not rashly incur any new dangers. It was a difficult decision for him: whether he should go forward to Rome or attempt to build up a new capital of his own at Capua. The decision was a matter of great debate then, and it has been discussed a great deal by military men in every age since his day. Right or wrong, Hannibal decided to establish his own capital at Capua and to leave Rome undisturbed.

He, however, sent immediately to Carthage for reinforcements. The messenger whom he sent was one of his generals named Mago. Mago made his way to Carthage with his tidings of victory and his bushel of rings, collected from the field of Cannae. The city of Carthage was greatly excited by the news which he brought. The friends and patrons of Hannibal were elated with enthusiasm and pride, and they taunted and reproached his enemies with the opposition to him they had manifested when he was originally appointed to the command of the army of Spain.

Mago met the Carthaginian senate, and in a very spirited and eloquent speech he told them how many glorious battles Hannibal had fought and how many victories he had won. He had contended with the greatest generals that the Romans could bring against him and had conquered them all. He had slain, he said, in all, over two hundred thousand men. All Italy was now subject to his power; Capua was his capital, and Rome had fallen. He concluded by saying that Hannibal was in need of considerable additional supplies of men and money and provisions, which he did not doubt the Carthaginians would send without delay. He then produced before the senate the great bag of rings which he had brought and poured them upon the pavement of the senate house as a trophy of the victories which he had announced.

This would, perhaps, have all been very well for Hannibal if his friends had been content to leave the case where Mago left it; but some of them could not resist the temptation of taunting his enemies, and especially Hanno, who, as will be recollected, originally opposed his being sent to Spain. They turned and asked him triumphantly what he thought now of his factious opposition to so brave a warrior. Hanno rose. The senate looked toward him and was profoundly silent, wondering what he would have to reply. Hanno, with an air of perfect ease and composure, spoke somewhat as follows:

"I would have said nothing and allowed the senate to take what action they pleased on Mago's proposition if I had not been particularly addressed. As it is, I will say that I think now just as I always have thought. We are plunged into a most costly and most useless war and are, as I believe, no nearer the end of it now than ever, notwithstanding all these boasted successes. The emptiness of them is clearly shown by the inconsistency of Hannibal's claims as to what he has done, with the demands that he makes in respect to what he wishes us to do. He says he has conquered all his enemies, and yet he wants us to send him more soldiers. He has reduced all Italy—the most fertile country in the world—to subjection and reigns over it at Capua, and yet he calls on us for corn. And then, to crown all, he sends us bushels of gold rings as a specimen of the riches he has obtained by plunder and accompanies the offering with a demand for new supplies of money. In my opinion, his success is all illusive and hollow. There seems to be nothing substantial in his situation except his necessities and the heavy burdens upon the state which these necessities impose."

In spite of Hanno's sarcasms, the Carthaginians resolved to sustain Hannibal and to send him the supplies
that he needed. They were, however, long in reaching him.
Various difficulties and delays occurred. The Romans,
though they could not remove Hannibal from his position in Italy, raised armies in different countries and waged
extended wars with the Carthaginians and their allies in
various parts of the world, both by sea and land.

The result was that Hannibal remained fifteen or six-
teen years in Italy, engaged in a lingering struggle with the
Roman power during all this time, without ever being able
to accomplish any decisive measures. During this period
he was sometimes successful and victorious, and sometimes he was harassed by his enemies. It is said that his
army was indifferent and weakened by the comforts and
luxuries they enjoyed at Capua. Capua was a very rich and
beautiful city, and the inhabitants of it had opened their
gates to Hannibal of their own accord, preferring, as they
said, his alliance to that of the Romans. The officers—as
the officers of an army almost always do, when they find
themselves established in a rich and powerful city, after the
fatigues of a long and honorable military operation—gave
themselves up to festivities and rejoicing, to games, shows,
and entertainments of every kind, which they soon learned
to prefer much more than the toil and danger of marches
and battles.

Whatever may have been the cause, there is no question
about the fact that, from the time Hannibal and his army
got possession of their comfortable quarters in Capua, the
Carthaginian power began to gradually decline. As Hannibal decided to make that city the Italian capital instead
of Rome, he felt in some degree settled and at home, and
was less interested than he had been in plans for attacking

the ancient capital. Still, the war went on; many battles were fought, many cities were besieged, the Roman power gaining ground all the time, though not by any very decisive victories.

In these contests, after awhile, there appeared a new Roman general named Marcellus, and either on account of his possessing a bolder and more active personality or else in consequence of the change in the relative strength of the two contending powers, he pursued a more aggressive policy than Fabius had thought it wise to attempt. Marcellus was, however, cautious and wary in his ventures, and he laid his plans with so much sound judgment and skill that he was almost always successful. The Romans applauded his work and intense devotion, without, however, forgetting their obligations to Fabius for his caution and defensive reserve. They said that Marcellus was the sword of their commonwealth, as Fabius had been its shield.

The Romans continued to follow this sort of warfare, being more and more successful the longer they continued it, until, at last, they advanced to the very walls of Capua and threatened it with a siege. Hannibal's fortifications were too strong for them to attempt to carry the city by a sudden assault, and the Romans were not powerful enough to take the place entirely and completely shut their enemies in. They, however, camped with a large army in the neighborhood and assumed so threatening an attitude as to keep Hannibal's forces in a state of continual alarm. Besides their alarm, it was very humiliating and mortifying to Carthaginian pride to find the very seat of their power shut up and subdued by an enemy over whom they had been triumphing so short a time before.

Hannibal was not in Capua at the time the Romans came to attack it. He marched, however, immediately to its relief and attacked the Romans, attempting to compel them to raise the siege and withdraw. They had, however, so barricaded themselves in the positions they had taken, and had lost so much of their former force, that he could accomplish nothing decisive. He then left the ground with his army and marched toward Rome. He camped in the vicinity of the city and threatened to attack it; but the walls and castles and towers with which Rome, as well as Capua, was defended, were too formidable and the preparations for defense too complete to make it wise for him really to attack the city. His object was to alarm the Romans and compel them to withdraw their forces from his capital that they might defend their own.

There was, in fact, some degree of alarm awakened, and in the discussions which took place among the Roman authorities, the withdrawal of their troops from Capua was proposed; but this proposal was overruled and even Fabius was against it. Hannibal was no longer to be feared. They ordered back a small detachment from Capua and added to it such forces as they could raise within the city and then advanced to give Hannibal battle. The preparations were all made for a battle, but a violent storm came on, so violent as to drive the combatants back to their respective camps. This happened, the great Roman historian gravely says, two or three times in succession; the weather immediately became calm each time, as soon as the respective generals had withdrawn their troops from the intended fight. Something like this may perhaps have occurred, though the fact doubtless was that both parties were afraid, each of the other, and were disposed to allow themselves any excuse to postpone a decisive conflict. There was a time when Hannibal had not been deterred from attacking the Romans even by the most turbulent of storms.

Though Hannibal did, in the end, get to the walls of Rome, he did nothing but threaten when he was there, and his camp near the city could only be considered as bravado. His presence seemed to excite very little apprehension within the city. The Romans had, in fact, before this time, lost their terror of the Carthaginian arms. To show their contempt of Hannibal, they sold, at public auction, the land on which he was camped, while he was on it besieging the city, and it brought the usual price. The bidders were, perhaps, influenced somewhat by a patriotic spirit and by a desire to taunt Hannibal with an expression of their opinion that his occupation of the land would be a very temporary problem. Hannibal, to exact punishment for this taunt, put up for sale at auction, in his own camp, the shops of one of the principal streets of Rome, and they were bought by his officers with great spirit. It showed that a great change had taken place in the nature of the contest between Carthage and Rome, to find these vast powers, which were a few years before grappling each other with such destructive and terrible fury on the Po and at Cannae, now satisfying their declining animosity with such petty quarrels as this.

When the other methods by which Hannibal attempted to obtain reinforcements failed, he made an attempt to have a second army brought over the Alps under the command of his brother Hasdrubal. It was a large army, and in their march they experienced the same difficulties, though in a much lighter degree than Hannibal had himself encountered. And yet, of the whole mighty mass which set out from Spain, nothing reached Hannibal except his brother's head. The circumstances of the unfortunate end to Hasdrubal's attempt were as follows.

When Hasdrubal descended from the Alps, rejoicing in the successful manner in which he had made it through those formidable barriers, he imagined that all his difficulties were over. He dispatched couriers to his brother Hannibal, informing him that he had scaled the mountains and that he was coming on as rapidly as possible to his aid.

The two consuls in office at this time were named Nero and Livius. To each of these, as was usual with the Roman consuls, was assigned a particular province and a certain portion of the army to defend it, and the laws prohibited them, very strictly, from leaving their respective provinces, on any pretext whatever, without authority from the Roman Legislature. In this instance, Livius had been assigned to the northern part of Italy and Nero to the southern. It fell upon Livius, therefore, to meet and give battle to Hasdrubal on his descent from the Alps and to Nero to remain in the vicinity of Hannibal to thwart his plans, oppose his progress, and if possible, conquer and destroy him, while his colleague prevented his receiving the expected reinforcements from Spain.

Things being in this state, the couriers Hasdrubal sent with his letters had the vigilance of both consuls to elude before they could deliver them into Hannibal's hands. They did succeed in passing Livius, but they were intercepted by Nero. The patrols who seized the messengers brought them to Nero's tent. Nero opened and read the letters. All Hasdrubal's plans and arrangements were fully detailed in them. Nero believed that, if he were to proceed immediately to the north with a strong force, he could render assistance to his colleague. With the knowledge of Hasdrubal's plans he would probably be able to defeat him; whereas, if he were to leave Livius in ignorance and alone, he feared that Hasdrubal would be successful in breaking his way through and ultimately securing his reinforcement of Hannibal. Under these circumstances, he was, of course, eager to go northward to render the necessary assistance, but he was strictly forbidden by law to leave his own province to enter that of his colleague without an authority from Rome, which there was not now time to obtain.

The laws of military discipline are very strict and necessary, and in theory they are never to be disobeyed. Officers and soldiers, of all ranks and stations, must obey the orders which they receive from the authority above them, without considering the consequences or deviating for any excuse whatever. It is, in fact, the very essence of military subordination and efficiency that a command, once given, suspends all exercise of judgment or discretion on the part of the one to whom it is addressed.

And yet there are cases of exception—cases where the necessity is so urgent or the advantages so great; where the interests involved are so momentous and the success so sure that a commander chooses to disobey and take the responsibility. The responsibility is very great, and the danger in assuming it extreme. He who incurs it makes himself liable to the most severe penalties from which nothing but clear proof of the most urgent necessity, and the most triumphant success, can save him. There is somewhere in English history a story of a naval commander, in the service of an English queen, who disobeyed the orders of his superiors at one time, in a case of great emergency at sea, and by doing so gained a very important victory. Immediately afterward he placed himself under arrest and went into port as a prisoner accused of crime instead of a commander triumphing in his victory. He surrendered himself to the queen's officers of justice and sent word to the queen herself that he knew very well that death was the penalty for his offense but that he was willing to sacrifice his life in any way in the service of her majesty. He was pardoned!

Nero, after much anxious deliberation, concluded that the emergency in which he found himself placed was one requiring him to take the responsibility of disobedience. He did not, however, dare to go north with all his forces, for that would be to leave southern Italy totally at the mercy of Hannibal. He selected, therefore, from his whole force, which consisted of forty thousand men, seven or eight thousand of the most efficient and trustworthy—the men on whom he could most securely rely, both in respect to their ability to bear the fatigue of a rapid march, and the courage and energy with which they would meet Hasdrubal's forces in battle. He was, at the time when Hasdrubal's letters were intercepted, occupying a spacious and well-situated camp. This he enlarged and strengthened so that Hannibal might not suspect that he intended any reduction of the forces within. All this was done very promptly, so that, in a few hours after he received the news on which he was acting, he was drawing off secretly at night a column of six or eight thousand men, none of whom knew where they were going.

He proceeded as rapidly as possible to the north, and when he arrived in the Northern Province, he planned to get into the camp of Livius as secretly as he had got out from his own. Therefore, of the two armies, the one where an increase of force was required was greatly strengthened at the expense of the other without either of the Carthaginian generals having suspected the change.

Livius rejoiced to get so opportune a reinforcement. He recommended that the troops all remain quietly in camp for a short time, until the newly arrived troops could rest and restore themselves a little after their rapid and fatiguing march; but Nero opposed this plan and recommended an immediate battle. He knew the character of the men that he had brought, and besides, he was unwilling to risk the dangers which might arise in his own camp, in southern Italy, by too long an absence from it. It was decided to attack Hasdrubal at once, and the signal for battle was given.

It is possible that Hasdrubal could have been beaten by Livius alone, but the additional force which Nero brought made the Romans altogether too strong for him. Besides, from his position in the front of the battle, he believed, from some indications that his watchful eye observed, that a part of the troops attacking him were from the south; and he speculated from this that Hannibal had been defeated and that, in consequence of this, the whole united force of the Roman army was coming against him. He was disheartened and discouraged and soon ordered a retreat. He was pursued by the various divisions of the Roman army, and the retreating columns of the Carthaginians were soon thrown into complete confusion. They became entangled among rivers and lakes; and the guides who had undertaken to escort the army, finding that all was lost, abandoned them and fled, anxious only to save their own lives. The Carthaginians were soon confined in a position where they could not defend themselves and from which they could not escape. The Romans showed them no mercy, and went on killing their wretched and despairing victims until the whole army was almost totally destroyed. They cut off Hasdrubal's head, and Nero set out the very night after the battle to return with it in triumph to his own camp. When he arrived, he sent a troop of horsemen to throw the head over into Hannibal's camp, a ghastly and horrid trophy of his victory.

Hannibal was overwhelmed with disappointment and sorrow at the loss of his army, bringing with it, as it did, the destruction of all his hopes. "My fate is sealed," he said. "All is lost. I shall send no more news of victory to Carthage. In losing Hasdrubal my last hope is gone."

While Hannibal was in this condition in Italy, the Roman armies, aided by their allies, were gaining gradually against the Carthaginians in various parts of the world, under the different generals who had been placed in command by the Roman senate. The news of these victories came continually back to Italy and encouraged and excited the Romans, while Hannibal and his army, as well as the people who were in alliance with him, were disheartened and depressed by them. Scipio was one of these generals commanding in foreign lands. His province was Spain. The news which came home from his army became more and more exciting, as he advanced from conquest to conquest, until it seemed that the whole country was going to be reduced to subjection. He overcame one Carthaginian general after another until he reached New Carthage, which he besieged and conquered, and the Roman authority was established fully over the whole land.

Scipio then returned in triumph to Rome, and the people received him with shouts of exultation. At the next election they chose him as consul. On the allotment of provinces, Sicily fell to him, with power to cross into Africa if he pleased. The war in Italy, more directly against Hannibal, was passed on to the other consul to carry on. Scipio levied his army, equipped his fleet, and sailed for Sicily.

The first thing he did on arrival in his province was to send an expedition into Africa. He could not face Hannibal directly by marching his troops into the south of Italy, for this was the work allotted to his colleague. With

the boldness and fervor which marked his character he
decided to make an incursion into Africa and even threaten
Carthage itself.

He was triumphantly successful in all his plans. His
army went on from victory to victory, filled with enthusiasm and confident of success as his forces in Spain had
been. They conquered cities, they overran provinces, they
defeated and drove back all the armies which the Carthaginians could bring against them, and finally they awakened
in the streets and dwellings of Carthage the same panic that
Hannibal's victorious progress had produced in Rome.

The Carthaginians being now reduced to despair, sent
ambassadors to Scipio to beg for peace and to ask on what
terms he would grant it and withdraw from the country.
Scipio replied that *he* could not make peace. It rested with
the Roman senate, whose servant he was. He specified,
however, certain terms which he was willing to propose to
the senate, and if the Carthaginians would agree to them,
he would grant them a truce, a temporary suspension of
hostilities until the answer of the Roman senate could be
returned.

The Carthaginians agreed to the terms. They were very
troubled. The Romans say that they did not really mean
to abide by them but agreed in order to gain time to send
for Hannibal. They had great confidence in his resources
and military power and thought that, if he were in Africa,
he could save them. At the same time they sent their ambassadors to Rome with their propositions for peace, they
dispatched messages to Hannibal, ordering him to send his
troops as soon as possible and, abandoning Italy, to hasten
home to save, if it was not already too late, his native city
from destruction.

When Hannibal received the messages, he was over-whelmed with disappointment and sorrow. He spent hours in extreme restlessness, sometimes in a moody silence, inter-rupted now and then by groans of despair, and sometimes uttering loud and angry curses, prompted by the exaspera-tion of his feelings. However, he could not resist. He made the best of his way to Carthage. The Roman senate, at the same time, instead of deciding on the question of peace or war, which Scipio had submitted to them, referred the question back to him. They sent commissioners to Scipio, authorizing him to act for them and to decide himself alone whether the war should be continued or closed, and if to be closed, on what conditions.

Hannibal raised a large force at Carthage, joining with it the remains of former armies left after Scipio's battles, and he went forward at the head of these troops to meet his ene-my. He marched five days, going seventy-five or one hundred miles from Carthage, when he found himself approaching Scipio's camp. He sent out spies to survey the enemy. The patrols of Scipio's army seized the spies and brought them to the general's tent, as they supposed, for execution. Instead of punishing them, Scipio ordered them to be led around his camp and to be allowed to see everything they desired. He then dismissed them that they might return to Hannibal with the information they had obtained.

The report they brought to Hannibal was that the strength and resources of Scipio's army made them a for-midable opponent. Hannibal thought it best to make an attempt to negotiate peace rather than to risk a battle, and he sent word to Scipio requesting a personal interview. Scipio agreed to this request, and a place was appointed for the meeting between the two camps. To this spot the two generals arrived at the proper time, with great splendor and parade and with many attendants. They were the two greatest generals of the age in which they lived, at the head of vast armies, having been engaged for fifteen or twenty years in performing exploits which had filled the world with their fame. Their fields of action had, however, been widely distant, and they met personally now for the first time. When introduced into each other's presence, they stood for some time in silence, gazing on and examining one another with intense interest and curiosity, but not speaking a word.

Finally, the negotiation was opened. Hannibal made Scipio proposals for peace. They were very favorable to the Romans, but Scipio was not satisfied with them. He demanded still greater sacrifices than Hannibal was willing to make. The result, after a long and fruitless negotiation, was that each general returned to his camp and prepared for battle.

In military operations, it is generally easy for those who have been conquering to go on to conquer: so much depends upon the expectations with which the contending armies go into battle. Scipio and his troops expected to conquer. The Carthaginians expected to be beaten. The result corresponded. At the close of the day on which the battle was fought, forty thousand Carthaginians were dead and dying on the ground, as many more were prisoners in the Roman camp, and the rest, in broken masses, were fleeing from the field in confusion and terror on all the roads which led to Carthage. Hannibal arrived at the city with the rest, went to the senate, announced his defeat, and said that he could do no more. "The fortune which once attended me," said he, "is lost forever, and nothing is left to us but to make peace with our enemies on any terms that they may think fit to impose."

CHAPTER XI

HANNIBAL A FUGITIVE
AND AN EXILE.

ANNIBAL'S life was like an April day. Its brightest glory was in the morning. The setting of his sun was darkened by clouds and showers. Although for fifteen years the Roman people could find no general capable of maintaining the field against him, Scipio conquered him at last, and all his brilliant conquests ended, as Hanno had predicted, only in placing his country in a far worse condition than before.

In fact, as long as the Carthaginians confined their energies to useful industry and to the pursuits of commerce and peace, they were prosperous, and they increased in wealth and influence and honor every year. Their ships went everywhere and were everywhere welcome. All the shores of the Mediterranean were visited by their merchants, and the comforts and the happiness of many nations and tribes were promoted by the very means which they took to swell their own riches and fame. All might have gone on like this for centuries longer had not military heroes arisen with appetites for a more appealing sort of glory. Hannibal's father was one of the foremost of these. He began by conquests in Spain and intrusion on the Roman powers. He instilled the same feelings of ambition and hate in Hannibal's mind which burned in his own. For many years, the policy which they led their countrymen to pursue was successful. From being useful and welcome visitors to the entire world, they became the masters and the curse of a part of it. So long as Hannibal remained superior to any Roman general that could be brought against him, he went on conquering. But at last Scipio arose, greater than Hannibal. The tide was then turned, and all the vast conquests of half a century were wrested away by the same violence, bloodshed, and misery with which they had been acquired.

We have described the exploits of Hannibal, in making these conquests, in detail, while those of Scipio, in wresting them away, have been passed over very briefly, as this is intended as a history of Hannibal and not of Scipio. Still, Scipio's conquests were made by slow degrees, and they consumed a long period of time. He was but about eighteen years of age at the battle of Cannae, soon after which his campaigns began, and he was thirty when he was made consul, just before going into Africa. He spent fifteen or eighteen years taking down the vast superstructure of power which Hannibal had raised, working in regions away from Hannibal and Carthage during all this time, as if leaving the great general and the great city for last. He was so successful in what he did that when he finally advanced to the attack of Carthage, everything else was gone. The Carthaginian power had become a mere hollow shell, empty and vain, which required only one great final blow to effect its absolute demolition. In fact, so far spent and gone were all the Carthaginian resources that the great city had to summon the great general to its aid the moment it was threatened, and Scipio destroyed them both together.

And yet Scipio did not proceed so far as literally and actually to destroy them. He spared Hannibal's life, and he allowed the city to stand; but the terms and conditions of peace which he exacted were such as to put an absolute and final end to Carthaginian dominion. By these conditions, the Carthaginian state was allowed to continue free and independent and even to retain the government of such territories in Africa as they possessed before the war; but all their foreign possessions were taken away, and even in respect to Africa, their jurisdiction was limited and curtailed by very hard restrictions. Their whole navy was to be given to the Romans except ten small ships of three banks of oars, which Scipio thought the government would need for the purposes of civil administration. These they were allowed to keep. Scipio did not say what he would do with the remainder of the fleet once it was unconditionally surrendered to him. The elephants of war were also to be given up and no longer trained. They were not to appear at all as a military power in any other quarter of the world but Africa, and they were not to make war in Africa except by previously making known the reason for it to the Roman people and obtaining their permission. They were also to pay to the Romans a very large annual tribute for fifty years.

There was great distress and uncertainty in the Carthaginian councils while they were debating these cruel terms. Hannibal was in favor of accepting them. Others opposed. They thought it would be better still to continue the struggle, hopeless as it was, than to submit to terms so humiliating and fatal.

Hannibal was present at these debates, but he found himself now in a very different position from that which he had occupied for thirty years as a victorious general at the head of his army. He had been accustomed to controlling and directing everything. In his councils of war, no one spoke but at his invitation, and no opinion was expressed but such as he was willing to hear. In the Carthaginian senate, however, he found the case very different. There, opinions were freely expressed as in a debate among equals, Hannibal taking his place among the rest and counting only as one. And yet the spirit of authority and command which he had been so long accustomed to exercise lingered still and made him very impatient and uneasy under contradiction. In fact, as one of the speakers in the senate was rising to comment unfavorably and oppose Hannibal's views, he undertook to pull him down and silence him by force. This awakened such immediate expressions of dissatisfaction and displeasure in the assembly as if to show him clearly that the time for such domineering was gone. He had, however, the good sense to express the regret he soon felt at having so far forgotten the duties of his new position, and to make a sufficient apology.

The Carthaginians finally decided to agree to Scipio's terms of peace. The first installment of the tribute was paid. The elephants and the ships were surrendered. After a few days, Scipio announced his determination not to take the ships away with him, but to destroy them there. Perhaps this was because he thought the ships would be of little value to the Romans, on account of the difficulty of manning them. Ships, of course, are useless without seamen, and many nations in modern times, who could easily build a navy, are hindered from doing it because their population does not furnish sailors in sufficient numbers to man and navigate it. It was probably, in part, on this account that Scipio decided not to take the Carthaginian ships away, and perhaps he also wanted to show to Carthage and to the world that his object in taking possession of the national property of his foes was not to enrich his own country by plunder but only to deprive ambitious soldiers of the power to compromise any longer the peace and happiness of mankind by expeditions for conquest and power. However this may be, Scipio decided to destroy the Carthaginian fleet and not to convey it away.

On a given day, therefore, he ordered all the galleys to be gathered together in the bay opposite to the city of Carthage and to be burned. There were five hundred of them, so that they constituted a large fleet and covered a large expanse of the water. A vast crowd of people assembled on the shores to witness the grand destructive fire. The emotion that such a spectacle was of itself expected to excite was greatly heightened by the deep but stifled feelings of resentment and hate which disturbed every Carthaginian breast. The Romans, as they gazed on the scene from their camp on the shore, were disturbed as well, though with different emotions. Their faces beamed with an expression of exultation and triumph as they saw the vast masses of flame and columns of smoke ascending from the sea, proclaiming the total and irretrievable ruin of Carthaginian pride and power.

Having fully accomplished his work, Scipio set sail for Rome. All Italy had been filled with the fame of his exploits in destroying the domination of Hannibal. The city of Rome had now nothing more to fear from its great enemy. He was shut up, disarmed, and helpless in his own native state, and the terror which his presence in Italy had inspired had passed away forever. The whole population of Rome, remembering the awful scenes of terror which the city had so often endured, regarded Scipio as a great deliverer. They were eager to receive and welcome him on his arrival. When the time came and he approached the city, vast crowds went out to meet him. The authorities formed civic processions to welcome him. They brought crowns and garlands and flowers and hailed his approach with loud and prolonged shouts of triumph and joy. They gave him the name of Africanus, in honor of his victories. This was a new honor—giving to a conqueror the name of the country that he had subdued; it was invented specially as Scipio's reward, the deliverer who had saved the empire from the greatest and most terrible danger by which it had ever been troubled.

Hannibal, though fallen, retained still in Carthage some portion of his former power. The glory of his past exploits still enveloped his character with a sort of halo, which made him an object of general regard, and he still had great and powerful friends. He was elevated to high office and exerted himself to regulate and improve the internal affairs of the state. In these efforts, however, he was not very successful. The historians say that the goals which he aimed to accomplish were good and that the measures he took were, in themselves, sensible; but, accustomed as he was to the authoritative and arbitrary action of a military commander in camp, he found it hard to practice that caution and self-control and respect for the opinion of others, which are so essential as means of influencing men in the management of the civil affairs of a commonwealth. He made a great many enemies, who did everything in their power, by plots and intrigues, as well as by open hostility, to accomplish his ruin.

His pride, too, was extremely mortified and humbled by an occurrence which took place very soon after Scipio's return to Rome. There was some reason for war with a neighboring African tribe, and Hannibal headed some forces which were raised in the city for the purpose and went out to undertake it. The Romans, who took care to have agents in Carthage to keep them updated with all that occurred, heard of this and sent word to Carthage to warn the Carthaginians that this was contrary to the treaty and could not be allowed. The government, not willing to incur the risk of another visit from Scipio, sent orders to Hannibal to abandon the war and return to the city. Hannibal was compelled to submit; but after having been accustomed for many years, to bid defiance to all the armies and fleets which Roman power could bring against him, it must have been very hard for such a spirit as his to find itself stopped and conquered now by a word. All the force they could command against him, even at the very gates of their own city, was once useless and vain. Now, a mere message and threat, coming across the distant sea, seeks him out in the remote deserts of Africa and in a moment deprives him of all his power.

Years passed away, and Hannibal, though compelled outwardly to submit to his fate, was restless and ill at ease. His scheming spirit, spurred on now by the double stimulus of resentment and ambition, was always busy, vainly trying to discover some plan by which he might again renew the struggle with his ancient foe.

It will be remembered that Carthage was originally a commercial colony from Tyre, a city on the eastern shores of the Mediterranean Sea. The countries of Syria and Phoenicia were in the vicinity of Tyre. They were powerful commercial communities, and they had always retained very friendly relations with the Carthaginian commonwealth. Ships passed continually to and fro, and always, in case of calamities or disasters threatening one of these regions, the inhabitants naturally looked to the other for refuge and protection—Carthage looked upon Phoenicia as its mother and Phoenicia regarded Carthage as her child. Now there was, at this time, a very powerful monarch on the throne in Syria and Phoenicia named Antiochus. His capital was Damascus. He was wealthy and powerful and was involved in some difficulties with the Romans. Their conquests, gradually extending eastward, had approached the confines of Antiochus's realms, and the two nations were on the brink of war.

Things being in this state, the enemies of Hannibal at Carthage sent information to the Roman senate that he was negotiating and plotting with Antiochus to combine the Syrian and Carthaginian forces against them and plunge the world into another general war. The Romans sent a delegation to the Carthaginian government to demand that Hannibal be removed from his office and given up to them a prisoner, in order that he might be tried on this charge.

These commissioners came to Carthage, keeping the object of their mission a profound secret, since they knew very well that if Hannibal should suspect its purpose, he would make his escape before the Carthaginian senate could decide upon the question of surrendering him. Hannibal was, however, too distrustful of them. He found out what they had planned and immediately decided on making his escape. He knew that his enemies in Carthage were numerous and powerful and that the animosity against him was growing stronger and stronger. He did not dare to trust to the result of the discussion in the senate but decided to flee.

He had a small castle or tower on the coast, about one hundred and fifty miles southeast of Carthage. He sent a message ordering a vessel to be ready to take him to sea. He also made arrangements to have horsemen ready at one of the gates of the city at nightfall. During the day he appeared freely in the public streets, walking with an unconcerned air, as if his mind was at ease, and giving to the Roman ambassadors, who were watching his movements, the impression that he was not planning an escape. Toward the close of the day, however, after walking leisurely home, he immediately made preparations for his journey. As soon as it was dark he went to the gate of the city, mounted the horse which was provided for him, and fled across the country to his castle. There he found the vessel ready which he had ordered. He boarded the vessel and put to sea.

There is a small island called Cercina at a little distance from the coast. Hannibal reached this island on the same day that he left his tower. There was a harbor there, where merchant ships were accustomed to come in. He found several Phoenician vessels in the port, some bound to Carthage. Hannibal's arrival produced a strong sense of discomfort there, and to account for his appearance among them, he said he was going as an ambassador from the Carthaginian government to Tyre.

He was now afraid that some of these vessels that were setting sail for Carthage might carry the news back of his having being seen at Cercina, and to prevent this, he schemed, with his characteristic cunning, the following plan: He sent word around to all the shipmasters in the port, inviting them to a great party which he was to give and asked, at the same time, that they would lend him the mainsails of their ships to make a great awning with which to shelter the guests from the dews of the night. The shipmasters, eager to witness and enjoy the festive scene which Hannibal's proposal promised them, accepted the invitation and ordered their mainsails to be taken down. Of course, this confined all their vessels to port. In the evening, the company assembled under the vast tent, made by the mainsails, on the shore. Hannibal met them and remained with them for a time. In the course of the night, however, when they were all in the midst of their drunken party, he stole away, boarded a ship, and set sail, and before the shipmasters could awake from the deep and prolonged slumbers which followed their wine, and rig their mainsails to the masts again, Hannibal was far out of reach on his way to Syria.

Meanwhile, there was great excitement in Carthage—the news that he was not to be found spread through city the day after his departure. Great crowds assembled before his house. Wild and strange rumors circulated in explanation of his disappearance, but they were contradictory and impossible, and only added to the overall excitement. This excitement continued until the vessels at last arrived from Cercina and made the truth known. Hannibal was, by this time, safe beyond the reach of all possible pursuit. He was sailing away successfully, so far as outward circumstances were concerned, but dejected and wretched in heart, toward Tyre. He landed there in safety, and was kindly received. In a few days he went into the city, and after various wanderings, reached Ephesus, where he found Antiochus, the Syrian king.

As soon as Hannibal's escape was made known in Carthage, the people of the city immediately began to fear that the Romans would consider them responsible for it and they would incur a renewal of Roman hostility. In order to avert this danger, they immediately sent a message to

Rome to make known the fact of Hannibal's flight, and to express the regret they felt on account of it, in hopes to save themselves from the displeasure of their formidable foes. It may at first view seem very ungenerous and ungrateful of the Carthaginians to abandon their general in this manner, in the hour of his misfortune and calamity, and to take part against him with enemies whose displeasure he had incurred only in their service and in executing their will. And this conduct of the Carthaginians would have to be considered as not only ungenerous, but extremely inconsistent. But it was not. The men and the influences which now opposed Hannibal's projects and plans had opposed them from the beginning; only, so long as he went on successfully and well, they were in the minority, and Hannibal's supporters and friends controlled all the public action of the city. But now that the bitter fruits of his ambition and of his totally unjustifiable intrusion on the Roman territories and Roman rights began to be realized, the party of his friends was overturned. The power reverted to the hands of those who had always opposed him, and in trying to keep him down when he was once fallen, their action, whether politically right or wrong, was consistent and cannot be considered ungrateful or treacherous.

One might suppose that all Hannibal's hopes and expectations of ever again facing his great Roman enemy would be now finally destroyed and that he'd finally give up his active hostility and content himself with seeking some refuge where he could spend the remainder of his days in peace, satisfied with securing, after such dangers and escapes, his own personal protection from the vengeance of his enemies. But it is hard to quell and subdue such an unconquerable persistence and energy as his. He was not ready to submit to his fate. As soon as he found himself at the court of Antiochus, he began to form new plans for making war against Rome. He proposed to the Syrian monarch to raise a naval force and put it under his charge. He said that if Antiochus would give him a hundred ships and ten or twelve thousand men, he would take the command of the expedition in person, and he did not doubt that he should be able to recover his lost ground and once more humble his ancient and formidable enemy. He would go first, he said, with his force to Carthage to get the cooperation and aid of his countrymen there in his new plans. Then he would make a descent upon Italy, and he had no doubt that he should soon regain the dominance there which he had formerly held.

Hannibal's design of going first to Carthage with his Syrian army was doubtless induced by his desire to put down the party of his enemies there and to restore the power to his supporters and partisans. In order to prepare the way most effectively for this, he sent a secret messenger to Carthage, while his negotiations with Antiochus were going on, to make known to his friends there the new hopes which he began to cherish and the new designs which he had formed. He knew that his enemies in Carthage would be watching very carefully for any such message; he therefore wrote no letters and committed nothing to paper which, on being discovered, might betray him. He explained, however, all his plans very fully to his messenger and gave him specific and careful instructions as to his manner of communicating them.

The Carthaginian authorities were indeed watching very vigilantly, and intelligence was brought to them, by their spies, of the arrival of this stranger. They immediately took measures to arrest him. The messenger, who was himself as watchful as they, got news of this and planned immediately to flee. However, he first prepared some papers and placards, which he posted up in public places, in which he proclaimed that Hannibal was far from considering himself finally conquered. He was, on the contrary, forming new plans for putting down his enemies in Carthage, resuming his former dominance there, and carrying fire and sword again into the Roman territories; and in the meantime, he urged the friends of Hannibal in Carthage to remain faithful and true to his cause.

The messenger, after posting his placards, fled from the city in the night and went back to Hannibal. Of course, the incident produced considerable excitement in the city. It aroused the anger and resentment of Hannibal's enemies and awakened new encouragement and hope in the hearts of his friends. However, it led to no immediate results. The power of the party which was opposed to Hannibal was too firmly established at Carthage to be easily shaken. They sent information to Rome of the coming of Hannibal's messenger to Carthage and of the result of his mission, and then everything went on as before.

In the meantime, the Romans, when they learned where Hannibal had gone, sent two or three ambassadors there to confer with the Syrian government in respect to their intentions and plans and to watch the movements of Hannibal. It was said that Scipio himself went to the embassy, and that he actually met Hannibal at Ephesus, and had several personal interviews and conversations with him there. An ancient historian gives a particular account of one of these interviews, in which the conversation turned, as it naturally would do between two such distinguished commanders, on military greatness and glory. Scipio asked Hannibal whom he considered the greatest military hero that had ever lived. Hannibal granted it to Alexander the

Great, because he had penetrated, with comparatively a very small number of Macedonian troops, into such remote regions, conquered such vast armies, and brought so boundless an empire under his power. Scipio then asked him who he was inclined to place next to Alexander. He said Pyrrhus. Pyrrhus was a Grecian general, who crossed the Adriatic Sea and made war, with great success, against the Romans. Hannibal said that he gave the second rank to Pyrrhus because he systematized and perfected the art of war and also because he had the power of awakening a feeling of personal attachment to himself on the part of all his soldiers and even of the inhabitants of the countries that he conquered, beyond any other general that ever lived. Scipio then asked Hannibal who came next in order, and he replied that he would give the third rank to himself. "And if," added he, "I had conquered Scipio, I would consider myself as standing above Alexander, Pyrrhus, and all the generals that the world ever produced."

Various other anecdotes are told of Hannibal during the time of his first appearance in Syria, all indicating the very high degree in which he was esteemed and the curiosity and interest that people everywhere had to see him. On one occasion, it happened that a vain and self-conceited orator, who knew little of war but from his own theoretic speculations, was haranguing an assembly where Hannibal was present, being greatly pleased with the opportunity of displaying his powers before so distinguished an auditor. When the discourse was finished, they asked Hannibal what he thought of it. "I have heard," he said in reply, "many old dotards in the course of my life, but this is, verily, the greatest dotard of them all."

Hannibal failed, notwithstanding all his perseverance, to obtain the means to attack the Romans again. He was unwearied in his efforts, but, though the king sometimes encouraged his hopes, nothing was ever done. He remained in that part of the world for ten years, striving continually to accomplish his aims, but every year he found himself further from the attainment of them. The hour of his good fortune and of his prosperity was obviously gone. His plans all failed, his influence declined, his name and renown were passing away. At last, after long and fruitless contests with the Romans, Antiochus made a treaty of peace with them and, among the articles of this treaty, was one agreeing to give up Hannibal into their power.

Hannibal decided to flee. The place of refuge which he chose was the island of Crete. He found that he could not remain there long. He had, however, brought with him a large amount of treasure, and when about to leave Crete, he was uneasy about this treasure, as he had some reason to fear that the Cretans were intending to seize it. He decided to come up with a plan—some scheme to enable him to get his gold away. The plan he adopted was this:

He filled a number of earthen jars with lead, covering the tops of them with gold and silver. These he carried, with great appearance of caution and concern, to the Temple of Diana, a very sacred building, and deposited them there, under very special guardianship of the Cretans, to whom, as he said, he entrusted all his treasures. They received their false deposit with many promises to keep it safely, and then Hannibal went away with his real gold cast in the center of hollow statues of brass, which he carried with him, without suspicion, as objects of art of very little value.

Hannibal fled from kingdom to kingdom, and from province to province, until life became a miserable burden. The hostility of the Roman senate followed him everywhere, harassing him with continual anxiety and fear and destroying all hope of comfort and peace. His mind was a prey to bitter recollections of the past and still more dreadful forebodings for the future. He had spent all the early days of his life inflicting the most terrible injuries on the objects of his merciless animosity and hate, although they had never injured him, and now, in the last of his days, it became his destiny to feel the pressure of the same terror and suffering inflicted upon himself. The hostility he feared was equal to that which he had exercised—perhaps made more intense mingled with resentment and revenge by those who felt it.

Finally, when Hannibal found that the Romans were hemming him in more and more closely and that the danger increased of his falling at last into their power, he had a potion of poison prepared and kept it always in readiness, determined to die by his own hand rather than to submit to be given up to his enemies. The time for taking the poison at last arrived. The wretched fugitive was then in Bithynia, a kingdom of Asia Minor. The King of Bithynia sheltered him for a time but finally agreed to give him up to the Romans. Hannibal, learning this, prepared to flee. But he found, on attempting his escape, that all the methods of exit from the palace which he occupied, even the secret ones which he had expressly planned to aid his flight, were taken possession of and guarded. Escape was, therefore, no longer possible, and Hannibal went to his apartment and sent for the poison. He was now an old man, nearly seventy years of age, and he was worn down and exhausted by his prolonged anxieties and sufferings. He was glad to die. He drank the poison and in a few hours ceased to breathe.

THE DESTRUCTION OF CARTHAGE.

THE consequences of Hannibal's reckless ambition, and of his totally unjustifiable aggression on the Romans to gratify it, did not end with his own personal ruin. The flame which he had kindled continued to burn until at last it accomplished the entire and irretrievable destruction of Carthage. This happened in a third and final war between the Carthaginians and the Romans, which is known in history as the Third Punic War. With a narrative of the events of this war, ending, as it did, in the total destruction of the city, we shall close this history of Hannibal.

It will be remembered that the war which Hannibal waged against Rome was the second in the series, the contest in which Regulus figured so prominently having been the first. The one whose history is now to be given is the third.

The three Punic wars extended over a period of more than one hundred years. Each successive contest in the series was shorter, but more violent and desperate than its predecessor, while the intervals of peace were longer. The first Punic war continued for twenty-four years, the second about seventeen, and the third only three or four. The interval between the first and second was twenty-four years, while between the second and third there was a sort of peace for about fifty years. The longer these warlike relations between the two countries continued and the more they both experienced the awful effects and consequences of their quarrels, the less inclined they were to renew such dreadful struggles, and yet, when they did renew them, they engaged in them with a redoubled energy of determination and a fresh intensity of hate. Therefore the wars followed each other at greater intervals, but the conflicts, when they came, were more and more desperate and merciless in character.

After the close of the second Punic war, there was a sort of peace for about fifty years. Of course, during this time, one generation after another of public men arose, both in Rome and Carthage, each successive group inheriting the suppressed animosity and hatred which had been cherished by their predecessors. Of course, as long as Hannibal had lived and had continued his plots and schemes in Syria, he was the means of keeping up a continual irritation among the people of Rome against the Carthaginian name. The government at Carthage disapproved of his acts and professed to be totally opposed to his designs, but then it was, of course, well-known at Rome that this was only because they thought he was not able to execute them. They had no confidence whatever in Carthaginian faith or honesty, so of course, there could be no real harmony or stable peace.

There gradually arose another source of dissension. To the west of Carthage lies a country called Numidia. This country was a hundred miles or more in breadth and extended back several hundred miles into the interior. It was a very rich and fertile region and contained many powerful and wealthy cities. The inhabitants were warlike, and were particularly celebrated for their cavalry. The ancient historians say that they used to ride their horses into the field without saddles, and often without bridles, guiding and controlling them by their voices and keeping their seats securely by the exercise of great personal strength and supreme skill. These Numidian horsemen are often alluded to in the narratives of Hannibal's campaigns and, in fact, in all the military histories of the times.

Among the kings who reigned in Numidia was one who had sided with the Romans in the second Punic war. His name was Masinissa. He became involved in some struggle for power with a neighboring monarch named Syphax, and while Masinissa had joined himself to the Romans, Syphax had joined the Carthaginians, each chieftain hoping, by this means, to gain assistance from his allies in conquering the other. Masinissa's patrons proved to be the strongest, and at the end of the second Punic war, when the conditions of peace were made, Masinissa's dominions were enlarged and the undisturbed possession of them settled to him, the Carthaginians being bound by specific stipulations not to interfere with him in any way.

In commonwealths like those of Rome and Carthage, there will always be two great parties struggling against each other for the possession of power. Each wishing to profit from every opportunity to oppose the other, and they consequently almost always take different sides in all the great questions of public policy that arise. There were two such parties at Rome, and they disagreed in respect to the course which should be pursued in regard to Carthage, one being generally in favor of peace, the other perpetually calling for war. In Carthage there was a similar dissension, the one side in the contest being desirous to make peace with the Romans and avoid battles with them, while the other party was very restless and uneasy under the pressure of the Roman power over them and continually attempting to promote feelings of hostility against their ancient enemies, as if they wished that war would break out again. The latter party was not strong enough to bring the Carthaginian state into an open rupture with Rome itself, but they succeeded at last in getting their government involved in a dispute with Masinissa and in leading out an army to give him battle.

Fifty years had passed away since the close of Hannibal's war. During this time, Scipio—that is, the Scipio who conquered Hannibal—had disappeared from the stage. Masinissa was very advanced in life, being over eighty years of age. However, he still retained the strength and energy which had characterized him in his prime. He drew together an immense army, and mounting, like his soldiers, bareback upon his horse, he rode from rank to rank, gave the necessary commands, and completed the arrangements for battle.

The name of the Carthaginian general on this occasion was Hasdrubal. This was a very common name in Carthage, especially among the friends and family of Hannibal. The bearer of it, in this case, may possibly have received it from his parents in honor of the brother of Hannibal, who lost his head. During the fifty years of peace which had elapsed, there was ample time for a child born after that event to grow up to full maturity. At any rate, the new Hasdrubal inherited the feeling of hatred to Rome which characterized his namesake. He and his party plotted to gain temporary dominion in Carthage, and they took advantage of their brief possession of power to renew, indirectly at least, the contest with Rome. They banished the rival leaders, raised an army, and Hasdrubal took command of it, and they went forth in great force to encounter Masinissa.

It was in a way very similar to this that Hannibal had started his war with Rome, by seeking first a quarrel with a Roman ally. Hannibal, it is true, had started his aggressions at Saguntum in Spain. Hasdrubal began at Numidia in Africa, but, with the exception of the difference of geographical locality, all appeared to be the same, and Hasdrubal very likely supposed that he was about to enter in to the same glorious career which had immortalized his great ancestor's name.

There was another similarity between the two cases; both Hannibal and Hasdrubal had strong parties opposed to them in Carthage in the initial stages of their ventures. In the present instance, the opposition had been violently suppressed, and the leaders of it banished; but still the elements remained, ready, in case of any disaster to Hasdrubal's arms, or any other occurrence tending to diminish his power, to rise at once and put him down. Hasdrubal had therefore a double enemy to contend against: one before him on the battlefield and the other, perhaps still more formidable, in the city behind him.

The parallel, however, ends there. Hannibal conquered at Saguntum, but Hasdrubal was entirely defeated in the battle in Numidia. The battle was fought long and desperately on both sides, but the Carthaginians were forced to yield, and they retreated in confusion to seek shelter in their camp. The battle was witnessed by a Roman officer who stood on a neighboring hill and looked down on the scene

with intense interest all day. It was Scipio—the younger—
who afterward became the principal actor in the terrible
scenes which were enacted in the war which followed. He
was then a distinguished officer in the Roman army and
was on duty in Spain. His commanding general had sent
him to Africa to obtain some elephants from Masinissa for
the use of the army. He came to Numidia for this purpose,
and as the battle between Masinissa and Hasdrubal came
while he was there, he remained to witness it.

This second Scipio was not, by blood, any relative of
the other, but he had been adopted by the elder Scipio's
son and received his name; so that by adoption he was a
grandson. He was, even at that time, a man of high consideration among all who knew him for his great energy and
efficiency of character, as well as for his sound judgment
and practical good sense. He occupied a singular position
at the time of the battle, such as very few great commanders have ever been placed in; for, as he himself was attached
to a Roman army in Spain, having been sent merely as a
military messenger to Numidia, he was a neutral in this
contest and could not properly take part on either side.
He had only to take his place on the hill and look down
on the awful scene as on a display arranged for his special
gratification. He spoke of it as if he were highly gratified
with the opportunity he enjoyed, saying that only two such
cases had ever occurred before where a general could look
down, in such a way, on a great battlefield and witness the
whole progress of the fight. He was greatly excited by the
scene, and he spoke particularly of the appearance of the
veteran Masinissa, then eighty-four years old, who rode all
day from rank to rank on a wild and impetuous charger,
without a saddle, to give his orders to his men and to encourage and excite them by his voice and his example.

Hasdrubal retreated with his forces to his camp as soon as the battle was over and fortified himself there, while Masinissa advanced with his army, surrounded the camp, and hemmed the imprisoned fugitives in. Finding himself in extreme and imminent danger, Hasdrubal sent to Masinissa to open negotiations for peace, and he proposed that Scipio act as a sort of umpire or mediator between the two parties to arrange the terms. Scipio was not likely to be a very impartial umpire; but still, his intervention would afford him, as Hasdrubal thought, some protection against any excessiveness on the part of his conqueror. The plan, however, did not succeed. Even Scipio's terms were found by Hasdrubal to be unacceptable. He required that the Carthaginians give to Masinissa a certain extension of territory. Hasdrubal was willing to agree to this. They were to pay him, also, a large sum of money. Hasdrubal agreed also to this. They were, moreover, to allow Hasdrubal's banished opponents to return to Carthage. This, by putting the party opposed to Hasdrubal once more into power in Carthage, would have been followed by his own fall and ruin; he could not consent to it. He remained, therefore, shut up in his camp, and Scipio, giving up the hope of any agreement, took the elephants which had been provided for him and returned across the Mediterranean to Spain.

Soon after this, Hasdrubal's army, worn out with hunger and misery in their camp, forced him to surrender on Masinissa's terms. The men were allowed to go free, but most of them perished on the way to Carthage. Hasdrubal succeeded in reaching a place of safety, but the power of his party was destroyed by the disastrous result of his enterprise, and since his exiled enemies were recalled in accordance with the treaty of surrender, the opposing party was immediately restored to power.

Under these new councils, the first measure of the Carthaginians was to impeach Hasdrubal on a charge of treason for having involved his country in such difficulties, and the next was to send a solemn message to Rome to acknowledge the fault of which their nation had been guilty, to offer to surrender Hasdrubal into their hands, as the principal author of the deed, and to ask what further satisfaction the Romans demanded.

In the meantime, before these messengers arrived, the Romans had been deliberating about what to do. The strongest party was in favor of urging on the quarrel with Carthage and declaring war. They had not, however, come to any positive decision. They received the message, therefore, without enthusiasm and made no direct reply. As to the satisfaction which the Carthaginians ought to render to the Romans for having made war on their ally contrary to the solemn covenants of the treaty, they said that it was a question for the Carthaginians themselves to consider. They had nothing at present to say on the subject. The deputies returned to Carthage with this reply, which, of course, produced great uneasiness and anxiety.

The Carthaginians were more and more desirous now to do everything in their power to avert the threatened danger of Roman hostility. They sent a new message to Rome, with still more humble professions than before. The delegation set sail from Carthage with very little hope of accomplishing the object of their mission. They were authorized, nevertheless, to make the most unlimited concessions and to submit to any conditions whatever to avert the calamity of another war.

But the Romans had been furnished with a reason for beginning hostilities again, and there was a strong party among them now who were determined to take advantage of this opportunity to entirely extinguish the Carthaginian power. War had been declared by the Roman senate soon after the first delegation had returned; a fleet and army had been raised and equipped, and the expedition had sailed. When, therefore, the delegation arrived in Rome, they found that the war, which it was the object of their mission to avert, had been declared.

The Romans, however, gave them audience. The ambassadors expressed their willingness to submit to any terms that the senate might propose for stopping the war. The senate replied that they were willing to make a treaty with the Carthaginians on the condition that the latter would surrender themselves entirely to the Roman power and bind themselves to obey such orders as the consuls, on their arrival in Africa with the army, would issue. The Romans, on their part, guaranteed that they would continue in the enjoyment of their liberty, their territorial possessions, and their laws. As proof of the Carthaginian honesty of purpose in making the treaty, and security for their future submission, they were required to give up to the Romans three hundred hostages. These hostages were to be young persons from the first families in Carthage, the sons of the men who were most prominent in society there, and whose influence might be used to control the action of the nation. The ambassadors considered these terms very difficult to bear. They did not know what orders the consuls would give them on their arrival in Africa, and they were required to put the commonwealth totally into their power. In the guarantee which the Romans offered them, their territories and their laws were to be protected, but nothing was said of their cities, their ships, or their arms and weapons of war. The agreement, if executed, would put the Carthaginian commonwealth totally at the mercy of their masters, in respect to all those things which were in those days most valuable to a nation as elements of power. Still, the ambassadors had been instructed to make peace with the Romans on any terms, and they agreed to them, though with great reluctance. They were especially opposed to the agreement in respect to the hostages.

This system, which prevailed universally in ancient times, of having the government of one nation surrender the children of the most distinguished citizens to that of another, as security for the fulfillment of its treaty stipulations, was a very cruel hardship to those who had to suffer the separation; but it would seem that there was no other security strong enough to hold such lawless powers as governments were in those days, to their word. Stern and rough as the men of those warlike nations often were, mothers were the same then as now, and they suffered quite as deeply in seeing their children sent away from them to a foreign land, in hopeless exile for many years; in danger too, continually, of the most cruel treatment and even of death itself, in retaliation for some alleged governmental wrong.

Of course the ambassadors knew, when they returned to Carthage with these terms, that they were bringing difficult news. When the news came, it threw the community into the most extreme distress. It is said that the whole city was filled with cries and shouts of sorrow. The mothers, who felt that their children would soon die, beat their breasts and tore their hair and manifested by every other sign their extreme and unrelieved distress. They begged and pleaded with the husbands and fathers not to consent to such cruel and intolerable conditions. They could not, and they would not give up their children.

The husbands and the fathers, however, felt compelled to resist all these pleas. They could not now undertake to resist the Roman will. Their army had been nearly destroyed in the battle with Masinissa; their city was, as a result, defenseless, and the Roman fleet had already reached its African port, and the troops were landed. There was no possible way, it appeared, of saving themselves and their city from absolute destruction, but by entire submission to the terms which their stern conquerors had imposed on them.

The hostages were required to be sent, within thirty days, to the island of Sicily, to a port on the western end of the island called Lilybaeum. Lilybaeum was the port in Sicily nearest to Carthage, being perhaps at a distance of a hundred miles across the waters of the Mediterranean Sea. A Roman escort would receive them there and take them to Rome. Although thirty days was allowed to the Carthaginians to select and send forward the hostages, they decided not to avail themselves of this offered delay, but to send the unhappy children forward at once that they might testify to the Roman senate, by this their promptness, that they desired to earn their favor.

The children were chosen, one from each of the leading families in the city, and three hundred in all. One can only imagine the heartrending scenes of suffering which must have devastated these three hundred families and homes, when the stern and unyielding edict came to each of them that one loved member of the household must be selected to go. And when, at last, the hour arrived for their departure, and they assembled on the pier, the picture was one of intense suffering. The poor exiles stood bewildered with terror and grief, about to part with all that they ever held dear—their parents, their brothers and sisters, and their native land—to go they knew not where, under the care of iron-hearted soldiers, who seemed to have no feelings of tenderness or compassion for their misery. Their inconsolable mothers wept and groaned aloud, clasping the loved ones who were about to be torn forever from them in their arms, in a storm of maternal affection and irrepressible grief. Their brothers and sisters, and their youthful friends stood by, some almost frantic with emotions which they did not attempt to suppress, others mute and motionless in their sorrow, shedding bitter tears of anguish, or gazing wildly on the scene with looks of despair. The fathers, whose stern duty it was to pass through this scene unmoved, walked back and forth restlessly, in deep but silent distress, spoke in broken and incoherent words to one another, and finally, by a mixture of persuasion and gentle force, drew the children away from their mothers' arms, and got them on board the vessels which were to take them away. The vessels made sail and passed off slowly from the shore. The mothers watched them until they could no longer be seen and then returned, hopelessly unhappy and miserable, to their homes; and then the grief of this parting scene was succeeded by the anxious suspense which now pervaded the whole city to learn what new dangers and indignities they were to suffer from the approaching Roman army, which they knew must now be well on its way.

The Roman army landed at Utica. Utica was a large city to the north of Carthage, not far from it, and on the same bay. When the people of Utica found that another serious clash was to take place between Rome and Carthage, they knew in advance what would most likely be the end of the contest. They decided that, in order to save themselves from the ruin which was plainly impending over the sister city, they must abandon her to her fate and make peace with Rome. They had sent deputies to the Roman senate, offering to surrender Utica to their power. The Romans accepted the submission and had made this city, in consequence, the port of entry for their army.

As soon as the news arrived at Carthage that the Roman army had landed at Utica, the people sent deputies to inquire about the orders of the consuls, for they had bound themselves by the treaty to obey the orders which the consuls were to bring. They found, when they arrived there, that the bay was covered with the Roman shipping. There were fifty vessels of war, of three banks of oars each, and a vast number of transports besides. There was, too, in the camp upon the shore, a force of eighty thousand foot soldiers and four thousand horsemen, all armed and equipped in the most perfect manner.

The deputies were convinced that this was a force which it was in vain for their countrymen to think of resisting. They asked, trembling, for the consuls' orders. The consuls informed them that the orders of the Roman senate were, first, that the Carthaginians furnish them with a supply of corn for their troops. The deputies went back to Carthage with the demand.

The Carthaginians complied. They were bound by their treaty and by the hostages they had given, as well as intimidated by the presence of the Roman force. They furnished the corn.

The consuls, soon after this, made another demand of the Carthaginians. It was that they surrender to them all their vessels of war. They were more unwilling to comply with this requirement than with the other, but they agreed at last. They hoped that the demands of their enemies would stop there and that, satisfied with having weakened them this far, they would go away and leave them; they could then build new ships again when better times should return.

But the Romans were not satisfied yet. They sent a third order, that the Carthaginians deliver up all their arms, military stores, and warlike machines of every kind, by sending them into the Roman camp. The Carthaginians were rendered almost desperate by this request. Many were determined that they would not submit to it but would resist at all hazards. Others despaired of all possibility of resisting now and gave up all as lost; while the three hundred families from which the hostages had gone, trembled for the safety of the captive children and urged compliance with the demand. The advocates for submission finally gained the day. The arms were collected and carried in an immeasurable long column of wagons to the Roman camp. There were two hundred thousand complete suits of armor, darts and javelins without number, and two thousand military engines for hurling beams of wood and stones. And Carthage was disarmed.

All these demands, however unreasonable and cruel as the Carthaginians deemed them, were only preliminary to the great final act, the announcement of which the consuls had reserved for the end. When the arms had all been delivered, the consuls announced to their now defenseless victims that the Roman senate had decided that Carthage was to be destroyed. They gave orders that the inhabitants must all leave the city, which, as soon as it was vacated, was to be burned. They were to take with them as much property as they could carry; and they were at liberty to build, in lieu of their fortified seaport, an inland town, not less than ten miles' distance from the sea, only it must have no walls or fortifications of any kind.

The announcement of this entirely unparalleled and intolerable act threw the whole city into a frenzy of desperation. They could not, and would not, submit to this.

The begging and pleading of the friends of the hostages were all silenced in the burst of indignation and anger which arose from the whole city. The gates were closed. The pavements of the streets were torn up, and buildings demolished to obtain stones, which were carried up on the walls to serve instead of weapons. The slaves were all liberated and stationed on the walls to aid in the defense. Everybody that could work at a blacksmith's furnace was employed in fabricating swords, spearheads, pikes, and such other weapons as could be formed with the greatest skill and speed. They used all the iron and brass that could be obtained and then melted down vases and statues of the precious metals and tipped their spears with an inferior pointing of silver and gold. In the same manner, when the supplies of flax and hempen twine for cordage for their bows failed, the beautiful sisters and mothers of the hostages cut off their long hair and twisted and braided it into cords to be used as bowstrings for propelling the arrows which their husbands and brothers made. In a word, the wretched Carthaginians had been pushed beyond the last limit of human endurance and had stirred themselves to a hopeless resistance in a sort of frenzy of despair.

As you will remember, after the battle with Masinissa, Hasdrubal lost all his influence in Carthage and was, to all appearances, hopelessly ruined. He had not, however, given up the struggle. He had planned to assemble the remnant of his army in the neighborhood of Carthage. His forces had been gradually increasing during this time, as those who were opposed to these concessions to the Romans naturally gathered around him. He was now in his camp, not far from the city, at the head of twenty thousand men. Finding themselves in so desperate a situation, the Carthaginians sent to him to come to their defense. He

very gladly obeyed the summons. He sent around to all
the territories still subject to Carthage and gathered fresh
troops and collected supplies of arms and of food. He advanced to the relief of the city. He compelled the Romans,
who were equally astonished at the resistance they met
with from within the walls and at this formidable onset
from without, to retreat a little and fortify themselves in
their camp, in order to secure their own safety. He sent
supplies of food into the city. He also formed a plan to
secretly fit up a great many fireships in the harbor, and
setting them in flames, let them drift down on the Roman
fleet, which was anchored in supposed security in the bay.
The plan was so skillfully managed that the Roman ships
were almost all destroyed. Therefore the face of the battle
had changed. The Romans found themselves disappointed
by their prey. They confined themselves to their camp and
sent home to the Roman senate for new reinforcements
and supplies.

In a word, the Romans found that, instead of having
only to complete, unresisted, the simple destruction of a
city, they were involved in what would, perhaps, prove to
be a serious and a prolonged war. The war did, in fact,
continue for two or three years—a horrible war, almost of
extermination, on both sides. Scipio came with the Roman
army, at first as a subordinate officer, but his bravery, his
cleverness, and the success of some of his almost imagina-
tive but impractical exploits, soon made him an object of
universal regard. At one time, a detachment of the army,
which, he succeeded in releasing from a situation of great
peril, testified their gratitude by braiding a crown of grass
and placing it upon his brow with great ceremony and loud
shouts of approval.

The Carthaginians did everything in the undertaking of this war that the most desperate heroic courage could do; but Scipio's cool, steady, and well-calculated plans made irresistible progress and hemmed them in at last, within narrower and narrower limits, by a steadily increasing pressure, from which they found it impossible to break away.

Scipio had erected a sort of harbor or pier upon the water near the city, on which he had built many large and powerful engines to tear down the walls. One night a large company of Carthaginians took torches, not lighted, in their hands, together with some sort of apparatus for striking fire, and partly by wading and partly by swimming, they made their way through the water of the harbor toward these machines. When they were sufficiently near, they struck their lights and set their torches on fire. The Roman soldiers who had been stationed to guard the machines were seized with terror at seeing all these flashing fires burst out suddenly over the surface of the water and fled in dismay. The Carthaginians set the abandoned engines on fire and then, throwing their now useless torches into the flames, plunged into the water again and swam back in safety. But all this desperate bravery did very little good. Scipio quietly repaired the engines, and the siege went on as before.

But we cannot describe in detail all the particulars of this prolonged and terrible struggle. We must pass on to the closing scene, which, as related by the historians of the day, is an almost incredible series of horrors. After an immense number had been killed in the assaults made on the city, besides the thousands and thousands who had died of famine and of the exposures and hardships occurring with such a siege, the army of Scipio succeeded in breaking

their way through the gates and gaining admission to the
city. Some of the inhabitants were now ready to contend
no longer but to cast themselves at the mercy of the conqueror. Others, furious in their despair, were determined
to fight to the last, not willing to give up the pleasure of
killing all they could of their hated enemies, even to save
their lives. They fought, therefore, from street to street,
retreating gradually as the Romans advanced, until they
found refuge in the citadel. One band of Scipio's soldiers
mounted to the tops of the houses, the roofs being flat, and
fought their way there, while another column advanced in
the same manner in the streets below. No imagination can
conceive the uproar and loud noise of such an assault on
a populous city—a horrid mingling of the shouted commands of the officers and of the shouts of the advancing
and victorious assailants, with the screams of terror from
frightened women and children and dreadful groans and
pleadings from men dying maddened with unsatisfied revenge and biting the dust in an agony of pain.

The more determined of the combatants, with Hasdrubal at their head, took possession of the citadel, which
was a quarter of the city situated on a building and strongly
fortified. Scipio advanced to the walls of this fortification
and set that part of the city on fire which lay nearest to
it. The fire burned for six days and opened a large area,
which afforded the Roman troops room to act. When the
troops were brought up to the area left vacant by the fire,
and the people within the citadel saw that their condition
was hopeless, there arose, as there always does in such
cases, the desperate struggle within the walls whether
to persist in resistance or to surrender in despair. There
was an immense mass, not far from sixty thousand, half
women and children, who were determined to go out to

surrender themselves to Scipio's mercy and beg for their lives. Hasdrubal's wife, leading her two children by her side, earnestly pleaded with her husband to allow her to go with them. But he refused. There was a body of deserters from the Roman camp in the citadel, who, having no possible hope of escaping destruction except by desperate resistance to the last, Hasdrubal supposed would never yield. He committed his wife and children to their charge, and these deserters, seeking refuge in a great temple within the citadel, bore the frantic mother with them to share their fate.

Hasdrubal's determination, however, to resist the Romans to the last, soon after this gave way, and he surrendered. He is accused of the most atrocious treachery in attempting to save himself, after excluding his wife and children from all possibility of escaping destruction. But the confusion and uproar of such a scene, the suddenness and violence with which the events succeed each other, and the tumultuous and uncontrollable mental pressure to which they give rise, deprive a man who is called to act in it of all sense and reason and exonerate him, almost as much, from moral responsibility for what he does, as if he were insane. At any rate, Hasdrubal, after shutting up his wife and children with a furious gang of desperadoes who could not possibly surrender, surrendered himself, perhaps hoping that he might save them after all.

The Carthaginian soldiers, following Hasdrubal's example, opened the gates of the citadel and let the conqueror in. The deserters were now made absolutely desperate by their danger, and some of them, more furious than the rest, preferring to die by their own hands rather than to give their hated enemies the pleasure of killing them, set the building in which they were shut up in on fire. The miserable residents ran for safely, half-suffocated by the smoke and scorched by the flames. Many of them reached the roof. Hasdrubal's wife and children were among the number. She looked down from the roof, the volumes of smoke and flame rolling up around her, and saw her husband standing below with the Roman general—perhaps looking, in terror, for his wife and children, amid this scene of horror. The sight of the husband and father in a position of safety made the wife and mother perfectly furious with resentment and anger. "Wretch!" she screamed, in a voice which raised itself above the noise, "do you seek to save your own life while you sacrifice ours? I cannot reach you, but I kill you now with the lives of your children." So saying, she stabbed her frightened sons with a dagger and hurled them down, struggling all the time against their insane mother's frenzy, into the nearest opening from which flames were ascending and then leaped in after them herself to share their awful doom.

The Romans, when they had gained possession of the city, took the most decisive measures for its complete destruction. The inhabitants were scattered into the surrounding country, and the whole territory was converted into a Roman province. Some attempts were afterward made to rebuild the city, and it was for a long time a place of peace and quiet, as men lingered mournfully there in huts that they built among the ruins. It, however, was gradually deserted, the stones crumbled and decayed, weeds grew up from the soil, and now there is nothing whatever to mark the spot where the city lay.

When Hannibal appeared on the stage, he found his country engaged peacefully and prosperously in trade with the various countries of the then known world and promoting everywhere the comfort and happiness of mankind.

He then brought about a plan to turn all these energies into military aggression, conquest, and war. He perfectly succeeded. We certainly have in his person and history all the marks and characteristics of a great military hero. He gained the most splendid victories, devastated many lands, impeded and stopped the commercial interchange which was carrying the comforts of life to so many thousands of homes, and spread, instead of them, everywhere, deprivation, want, and terror, with pestilence and famine to follow. He kept the country of his enemies in a state of continuous anxiety, suffering, and alarm for many years, and overwhelmed his own native land, in the end, in absolute and irresistible ruin. In a word, he was one of the greatest military heroes that the world has ever known.

more from Canon Press

IT was agreed that Caesar must be slain; but the time, the place, and the manner in which the deed should be performed were all yet undecided. Various plans were proposed in the meetings which the conspirators held; but there was one thing peculiar to them all, which was, that they all agreed the deed should be performed in the most open and public manner. With a stern and undaunted boldness, which has always been considered by mankind as the ultimate example, they decided that, in respect to the actual execution of the solemn judgment which they had pronounced, there would be nothing private or concealed. They thought over the various public situations in which they might find Caesar and where they might strike him down, only to select the one which would be most public of all. . . .

In this view of the subject, they decided that the chamber of the Roman Senate was the proper place, and the Ides of March, the day on which he was appointed to be crowned, was the proper time for Caesar to be slain.

JULIUS CAESAR
MAKERS OF HISTORY SERIES

CPSIA information can be obtained at www.ICGtesting.com
Printed in the USA
270629BV00001B/4/P